# SOME OF MY
# BEST FRIENDS

ALSO BY EMILY BERNARD

*Remember Me to Harlem:*
*The Letters of Langston Hughes*
*and Carl Van Vechten, 1925–1964*

Amistad

AN IMPRINT OF

HARPERCOLLINS*Publishers*

# SOME OF MY BEST FRIENDS

WRITINGS ON

INTERRACIAL FRIENDSHIPS

*Edited by*

Emily Bernard

HarperCollins books may be purchased for educational, business, or sales
promotional use. For information, please write: Special Markets Department,
HarperCollins Publishers Inc., 10 East 53rd Street, New York, NY 10022.

FIRST EDITION

Grateful acknowledgment is made to David Mura for the use of
his poem "The Remark," and to Suheir Hammad for the use
of her poem "Some of My Best Friends."

*Designed by Deborah Kerner / Dancing Bears Design*

Printed on acid-free paper

Library of Congress Cataloging-in-Publication Data

Some of my best friends : writings on interracial friendships / edited
by Emily Bernard—
1st ed.
p. cm.
ISBN 0-06-008276-3
1. Friendship—Case studies. 2. Race relations—Case studies.
I. Bernard, Emily.
HM1161.S66 2004
302.3'4—dc22
2003070857

04  05  06  07  08  BVG/RRD  10  9  8  7  6  5  4  3  2  1

FOR THE LATE
RICHARD NEWMAN,
A CONNOISSEUR
OF ALL THINGS INTERRACIAL

# ACKNOWLEDGMENTS

In a public presentation of the essay he wrote for this book, John Gennari said, "To write an essay about a friendship is necessarily to put that friendship in jeopardy—and to remember what made that friendship so essential in the first place." I want to thank all the contributors to this book for what they recovered and chanced to get us here. Their risks and recollections are our rewards.

In particular, I would like to acknowledge the debt this book and its editor owe to Elizabeth Alexander, Maurice Berger, Pam Houston, and Susan Straight. Friends indeed.

Faith Childs is much more than my agent, and I am grateful for the multiple ways in which I benefit from her generosity and experience. Charles Harris believed in this project in its earliest stages. Dawn Davis, you are an outstanding editor, and every page of this book bears the imprint of your wisdom, patience, and good humor. Darah Smith had answers and warm words, too. Sharony Green's creative vision is an inspiration.

Where would this book be without the exquisite editorial eyes that belong to Warren Bernard, Greg Bottoms, Ellie DesPrez, David Huddle, Major Jackson, Amor Kohli, Todd McGowan, Miranda Massie, Hilary Neroni, Davida Pines, Danzy Senna, and Laura Yow? The answer is unimaginable. Thank you—it's not enough, but it's a start.

Billy, I am enlivened by the model of your integrity, passion, and great big heart.

Maurice, your mind is a delight, your friendship a blessing.

Hilary, thank you for every lovely writing day, and for every day that turned out to be something even finer.

John, you said, Why not? With you, all is possible, every wild thing within reach.

*...the heart is raised*

*on a mess of stories,*

*and then it writes its own.*

—JOE WOOD,
"The Negro Problem and Other Tales,"
in *Blacks and Jews: Alliances and Arguments*

# CONTENTS

CROSSING THE LINE: AN INTRODUCTION
Emily Bernard .... 1

BI-BIM-BAP
Jee Kim .... 13

NEARER, MY GOD, TO THEE
John Gennari .... 32

SOME WHITE MEN
Elizabeth Alexander .... 54

CARTILAGE
Susan Straight .... 64

BATTLEFIELDS, OR IS FRIENDSHIP GREATER
THAN THE COLONIAL AND DOMINATING RACE
IDEOLOGIES OF HUNDREDS OF YEARS?
Luis Rodriguez .... 72

REPELLENT AFRO
Trey Ellis .... 83

WHEN WE WERE FRIENDS:
A GEOGRAPHY LESSON
Bill Ayers .... 96

# CONTENTS

IN MY HEART IS A DARKNESS
Michelle Cliff .... 117

SECRET COLORS
David Mura .... 129

THE VALUE OF THINGS NOT SAID:
SOME THOUGHTS ON INTERRACIAL FRIENDSHIP
Maurice Berger .... 157

GRINGO RESERVATIONS
Sandra Guzmán .... 168

ON THE POSSIBILITY-FILLED EDGE
OF THE CONTINENT
Pam Houston .... 178

AS MY FRIEND ZACHARY SAYS
KADDISH FOR HIS FATHER ...
Darryl Pinckney .... 189

WITH ME WHERE I GO
Somini Sengupta .... 204

SOME OF MY BEST FRIENDS
Suheir Hammad .... 216

ABOUT THE CONTRIBUTORS .... 219

# SOME OF MY
# BEST FRIENDS

# CROSSING THE LINE:
# AN INTRODUCTION

## Emily Bernard

My mother will deny this but it's true. As a kid, whenever—and I mean, *without* exception—I came home from school and complained about some girl bossing me around, she would look at me and ask, "Is she white?" "Yes," I would invariably admit. Point made, she would arch a knowing eyebrow, and I would understand the discussion was over. My mother grew up in Hazelhurst, Mississippi, and routinely endured the rocks and clumps of dirt white kids, sons of millworkers, would throw at her and her grandmother as they walked to the dry goods store. For historical reasons, among others, my mother believed white people were not to be trusted. You could hardly blame her.

Despite the lessons of her history, my mother tolerated the steady stream of white girls who came over to play with me, occasionally with pleasure and amusement, at other times with barely concealed irritation. Sometimes her irritation had to do with being the mother of three young children; sometimes it had to do with being the mother of three young black children who had exclusively white friends. On one occasion, my mother caught me imitating the speech pattern of one of my friends and said, "Emily, you are *not* a little white girl." I had no idea what she meant by this. I still don't. At school, black kids equated "acting white" with making good grades and speaking formal English. At home, doing well in school was everything, and my parents' English was impeccable, so that wasn't it. Now I think she meant only that there was a line she felt it necessary to preserve between her daughter and the white girls who surrounded her. Maybe it's a line that all Old World mothers want to maintain between their daughters and strange New World customs and citizens. Maybe it was a line only my mother could see.

In the new world of suburban, upwardly mobile Nashville, Tennessee, in the 1970s, whiteness was not the only thing that irritated my mother. Every so often, she would respond to the invitations issued by black society types and lug me and my brothers to a party or a brunch. At these events, my mother was demure and polite, which let me know she was not having a good time. My diagnosis was always confirmed by the caustic observations she would make about these gatherings in the car on the way back home. I imagine my mother would not have been able to say what she found harder to stomach: the haughty airs and superficial ambitions of the black society types, or the inevitable loneliness that she feared lay ahead for her children if they were left to their own devices. She wanted us to meet and befriend black children who were like us. I appreciated and sympathized with her conflict, but only up to a point. Because for me there was no choice. I preferred the white girls, hands down.

Sometimes the white girls would come over, but as frequently as I could, I would go to their houses, usually after some battle with my mother, who would chauffeur me there in stony silence. She was tough, but she could always be won over with the "I thought you said people should be judged by their character" argument. Some of the white girls whose houses I particularly liked to visit were not of admirable character, but I didn't discuss that with my mother, even though I was fairly sure she suspected as much. Why did I prefer the white girls with poor character? First, most of them had money, and they abused their parents' resources spectacularly. They watched all the television shows and ate all the food forbidden in my own household. A few of them called their parents by their first names, and all of them talked back. None of the white mothers admonished their daughters about how they carried themselves, reminding them stringently of all they were representing. No set of white parents shook their heads in grim silence as they watched news reports about another black man arrested. The white girls of poor character cursed their parents, made jokes about farting, and slammed doors. They were without shame. They were free.

My mother was right, of course. Sooner or later, the white girls would slip up. In general, the freer the white girl, the uglier the moment of revelation. During dinner at Cathy's house, her stepfather admonished her by saying, "Eat like a white person!" Cathy giggled; my face burned. Later, in her room upstairs, I summoned the courage to bring it up. "My stepfather's not a racist. He's just a jerk," she said by way of reassurance. I asked her, "What does he think about me?" She said, "You're different." I wanted Cathy's family to like me, but her stepfather scared and disgusted me. Not surprisingly, this friendship didn't last. She didn't say it, but I suspected my mother wasn't sorry to see her go.

I liked being different.

The white girls with fine character thought I was different, too. Rebecca was the smartest person in the third grade. She talked the most and the fastest. One day, she needed a pencil, and I timidly offered one. I still recall holding out that pencil with my heart in my throat. It is my earliest romantic memory.

One day at recess, I saw Rebecca at the fence that bordered the playground behind our school. She was talking to a little white girl who lived in a house on the other side. As I approached them, I recoiled. My mother had warned me about the "poor white trash," as she referred to them, on the other side of the fence. Even from a few feet away, I could see the girl's face was dirty. She looked wild to me, like an animal. But I swallowed my fear and moved forward. Rebecca was there, after all. I was safe.

As I got closer, the dirty white girl's eyes widened, and she backed away. I wanted to turn around, look behind me, even as I *knew* it was I who frightened her. "What's the matter?" Rebecca asked the girl. "It's her," she said, pointing at me. "My mother told me not to talk to black people." Rebecca looked me over quickly. "Oh, *Emily*. She's different." Nearly thirty years later, what I remember is how desperately I hoped Rebecca's words would quiet the dirty girl. I knew what she meant. She meant what other white friends meant when they would say to me over the years, "I just don't think of you as black." She meant it as a compliment. I took it. Still, I remember wondering what it was exactly that Rebecca saw when she looked at me.

In high school, I wanted to be different from the black girls, even though I didn't really know any of them because I never had classes with other black students. Tracking meant I was always in classes only with other "advanced" kids; tracking meant I was always the only one. Tracking was my cross, my salvation. In the neutral world of my books, I was safe. But tracking also meant that when Jennifer asked, during a history lesson, why black people weren't grateful for slavery, I sat there, burning, silent, alone.

Tracking was a double-edged sword. Humiliations in history class were followed by endless journeys through endless miles of hallway to my next class. For others, the hallways were opportunities for note passing, efficiently executed pranks at lockers. For me, these same hallways were treacherous, and left me feeling exposed in a way that I didn't in the classroom, where I had the armor of class itself, of being first. The hallways were democratic. Grades didn't matter, but there were tests to pass, all the same. I failed the hallway tests daily. Black kids hanging against lockers whispered, sometimes laughed. What was it today? My outfit? My hair? The way I walked? I tried to see myself as they saw me, and felt shame and self-contempt for trying so hard, for not trying at all. I can't remember a single instance of being called "Oreo," not because it never happened, but because it happened all the time. "Don't worry about those kids," my mother would say. "They can't do anything to you." Oh, but they did. They did everything.

The white kids looked through me.

One day, Verna stepped out of the mass of mocking black faces and asked for my lunch money. She was tall and skinny in an old-lady way, bent, with sandy brown hair and skin. She simply stood in my path and asked for money, saying hers had been stolen, her mother was sick; I can't remember. I was nearly grateful that she gave me a reason when she didn't have to. Nearly. It was curious to me that she chose to beg and not bully. I handed her money and wondered at this shift, how her menacing figure was suddenly soft and supplicating. It was a lie, and she knew that I knew. Just beneath her pitiful posture, I knew there was still a person who wanted to do me violence. As much as this knowledge scared me, it liberated me, too, because I felt the same desire. On days when she didn't ask for money, I walked by her in the hallway with a walk made stiff by this desire to hurt her, its magnitude rivaled only by my fear of being hurt by her. Ours was a connection thick with unacted-upon rage. My feelings caused me confusion and guilt. I knew I should feel sympathy, but didn't. I was nothing like her, I told myself, nothing.

Verna. Surreptitiously, I looked for her in the hallways and at lunch. On weekends, I thought about her. I never told any of my white friends about Verna. Not even my close girlfriends, the ones who sometimes embarrassed me with their perceptive but unsolicited sympathy for my social predicament at school. "They wouldn't understand," I told myself. I believed they wouldn't understand because they were white. I believed that, if I told them, they would look at Verna and see only a poor, bent, black girl, even though when I looked at Verna, that's what I saw, too. I didn't tell them because I couldn't have borne looking in their eyes and recognizing the pity and contempt that I, too, felt for Verna. Because where their disgust would distinguish them from the poor, bent, black girl, mine bound me to her. I had wanted to be different from her. But I wasn't. I was different from the white girls. Because Verna may have hated me, but she *saw* me. None of the white girls ever really did.

In my experience, being loved isn't the same thing as being seen.

\*    \*    \*

On August 7, 1994, a man who was severely mentally ill stabbed seven people in a coffee shop in New Haven. I was one of the seven. On August 8, 1994, I woke up in a hospital bed, and Helena, who is white, was somehow just there, managing doctors, nurses, visitors, everything. From somewhere deep in my morphine-induced haze, I felt something much more than gratitude. "How can I ever thank you for this?" I asked, woozily racking my brain for ways to do that. She looked at me sternly and said, "I'm not here for you. I'm here for me." She stayed for a week, got everything in order, and left. This is one of the greatest gifts anyone has ever given me.

What I love about Helena, whom I have known now for almost twenty years, has nothing to do with race, but with the nearly primal space of comfort and acceptance that her friendship provides for me always, without hesitation or exception. At the same time, what I love about Helena has everything to do with race. Her racial identity must necessarily be as central to her as mine is to me, after all, so that loving Helena means loving her whiteness, too. In particular, I often take great private pleasure in the fact that she is Jewish, and proudly imagine that our alliance is blessed by the tradition of the grand historical connection between blacks and Jews. If Helena feels a similar pleasure about my blackness, she does not describe it in the careful, anxious grammar of the dogmatic antiracist. Some of these dogmatic types I admire greatly. Some of them I find extremely tedious, particularly when they exhibit symptoms of the illness I call "Racial Tourette's," identifiable when the host is unable to speak about anything *other* than race when in the presence of a nonwhite person. Some of these people, even the ones who suffer from Racial Tourette's, are my friends.

Here's a story about the dangers of dogmatic antiracism: I am at a dinner party sitting across the table from two white people, a man and a woman, who are talking about racism. "There's racism and then there's racism," the man says, and begins a story about a writer friend of his, a recent transplant to New York from an all-white Midwestern city. "He's not a racist but he's sometimes very clumsy," the man explains as he ends a story about his friend's most recent awkward interracial encounter, which involved his approaching a black woman from Louisiana at a social event and asking her which of the black "revival" churches in New York she attended. The woman was a Buddhist.

The man rolls his eyes and laughs. He says, "My friend's got a good heart, and he's eager to learn." He looks at the woman, who frowns and sighs. For long, uncomfortable seconds, they are both silent. Finally, the woman says coolly, "Well, it's not my job to educate people like that," and turns away.

The man is my husband, John, and the woman is Margaret, a civil rights lawyer, a committed antiracist, and an acquaintance of ours. In some ways, I respect the rigid lines Margaret draws between herself and other white people. She doesn't tolerate slippage, and polices the exact boundaries around her ideological commitments with a formidable vigilance. Let's be honest: The kind of fuzziness that decorates my own attitudes about race would never have gotten any important movement off the ground. But there is something missing from Margaret's racial repertoire, and it's the same thing that accounts for my friendship with the awkward writer in the first place: compassion. The writer sometimes sticks his foot in his mouth, but he is unfailingly compassionate. Where is the compassion in the rigid march of the sentry around and around her intractable borders between right and wrong? Ultimately, I believe that the boundaries serve the sentry, and no one else.

In general, I don't care if the white people I meet call themselves antiracists, or even have the "right" politics, which is a hard and fast friendship criterion for some who are dear to me. Right politics or not, some of my best friends, much like my mother, would never reveal their truest selves to a white person under any circumstances. Myself, I prefer to be knocked senseless by love, the fabled, blind kind of love that makes you want to give everything away. But then, I was thusly besotted with a woman named Susan, until the day she asked me what "the black community" really thought about names like Sheniqua and Tyronda, because "the white community" thought they were just bizarre. As she asked me this question, I watched myself turn, in Susan's eyes, from Emily into "the black community." And I watched her transform herself from Susan into someone who forgot, for a moment, that we had spent hours talking on the phone about our uncanny similarities, down to the cadence of our speech. Completely alike, we said. Completely understood, I felt. It was just a moment, but it changed everything. By the time I got up the nerve to bring it up, it was too late, mostly because I waited for two years, trying to forget it.

Blind love has its drawbacks.

When I told my friend Antonia, who is white and a committed antiracist, about Susan, I could feel her shudder all the way from California. When I send her a draft of this essay, she finds the part about antiracists insulting and simplistic, and I wonder if I didn't write it, in part, to irritate her. When I describe to her my discomfort with Margaret, she asks me to elaborate. I do so by quoting something Toni Morrison told Ed

Bradley on *60 Minutes* in 1998. Describing her dominant feelings about white people, Morrison said, "If the trucks pass and they have to make a choice, they'll put me on that truck."

"Margaret would never put you on the truck," Antonia says. "Maybe not," I fire back, "but she would put the first white person on it, just to say she did." We howl with laughter, and then we are back to business. Antonia insists that it is Margaret's personality and not her politics, that I find obnoxious. In addition, she thinks the head/heart dichotomy I have created with my competing stories about Margaret and Helena is facile. I tell her that while her politics may not be as righteous as Margaret's (here Antonia interrupts to voice her objections to the word "righteous"—she interrupts a lot), I know in my heart that Helena would never, under any circumstances, put me, or anyone else, on one of those trucks. I tell her these distinctions may be facile, but it's what I experience, and thank you very much for calling my experience facile. We argue about this for days, for weeks. It is not lost on me that I enjoy arguing with Antonia; it is one of the reasons that I love her so dearly. As she talks, I remember a discussion we had years ago about whether the phrase "white-knuckle it" was racially exclusionary. Our discussion spooled out into a ridiculous argument that ended with her hanging up on me. When she called back in the middle of the night, she said quietly, "I think the problem is that I expect a great deal of myself when it comes to these kinds of issues." I was moved and disarmed by her honesty, the deep level of comfort and acceptance between us she must have felt to make such an admission to me. I said, "I think it must be hard to be the kind of white person you are, because the kind of black person I am expects a great deal from you, too."

Since that night, I have used the phrase "white-knuckle it" every chance I get, and always think of Antonia when I do.

Helena wasn't the only person who came to be with me in the hospital. Antonia was there, too. In fact, my hospital room was bounteous with people, many of them white. These people I love for reasons both sensible and mysterious. They are my friends.

Friends. In the opening pages of *Maus: A Survivor's Tale*, by Art Spiegelman, Artie cries to his father, a Holocaust survivor, about hurts inflicted by his friends. His father responds, "Friends? Your friends? If you lock them together in a room with no food for a week, then you could see what it is, friends!"

I read these words and I see my mother's arched, knowing eyebrow.

You may always be right about the line between me and the white girls, Mom, but I believe in crossing it, all the same.

Conceiving this book was easy. It began with questions that have occupied me since childhood. Which ingredients make interracial friendships possible? Which factors destroy them? At what point does unintentional racial ungainliness become willful racist insensitivity? What do other people do at those moments when racial difference rears its head uncomfortably in a friendship? The older I became, the more questions I had. President Clinton inspired more when, after the 1992 Los Angeles uprising, he told the Democratic Leadership Council that "too many white Americans still simply have no friends of other races," and that, in part, was the cause of the city's turbulence. Could individual friendships be the answer to some of our larger social problems? If so, then how much should our intimate lives be shaped by our ideological beliefs? A book may be in order, I thought. I turned to writers I admired who had different histories and perspectives and asked them to reflect upon their particular experiences with interracial friendships. This book contains answers to my questions, and maybe yours, too.

Some writers in this collection focused on single relationships while others chose to chronicle the impact that certain types of interactions have had on the way they live in the world. Each story is distinct. Even in narratives written by people whose histories bear ostensible similarities, whole worlds of difference unfold in tone and language. At the same time, all these stories have an important quality in common, and that is an unwavering commitment to representing the painful, beautiful realities of friendships complicated by race and history. Every life, every vision represented here asks something new of you.

Conceiving this book was easy, but composing it was not. All the writers who contributed to this anthology dug deep to give you the pages that follow. What they came up with were portraits of intimacy, betrayal, loyalty, pain, joy, disappointment, and perseverance. These stories are about race, and they are not about race at all. They look like yours, and they are nothing like them. They will make you wonder, and despair, and worry, and remember, and forget, and laugh out loud. They will show you how to make friendships, interracial and otherwise, and how to lose them, too. They are hopeful and cynical; they are gloomy and promising. Together, they reveal all the messy, glorious, baffling things the heart needs, and the lengths, absurd and effortless, we must travel to get them.

# BI-BIM-BAP

## Jee Kim

Everything is real. Please believe me. Everything you're about to read is real.

It happened to Jee, who is essentially me, a Korean immigrant from a middle-class Seoul family who ended up in rural housing projects in Maryland populated by black families from a local military base and brown and yellow ones who worked in a nearby shoe factory. They later moved to Philly and opened a sneaker store on Frankford Avenue. But Jee's family didn't own a store in the ghetto and live out in the suburbs like a lot of other Koreans; they didn't have the money for that. So Jee grew up in the ghetto, feeling kinship being called nigga and gook by black kids and feeling fear and hate being called chink by the white kids at his magnet school.

It happened to Jee, or it happened to Chous, a half-Korean, half-black kid whose mom met her husband at an army base near Seoul and traded her life for a plane ticket, U.S. citizenship, and black eyes on the regular. When the beatings became too much, Chous's mom, who worked in Jee's family's sneaker store, left with her son. Jee's mom let them move in for a few months out of Korean love and Christian pity. She felt sorry for Chous not knowing his roots and tried to teach him Korean.

She also asked Jee to act like an older brother, but no one could influence or control Chous like that. Jee and Chous became childhood best friends. Like Jee, Chous identified more with the blacks and Ricans who he grew up with than the surburban Asians who shared half an ethnicity, only in words.

It happened to Jee, or it happened to Six, a third-generation Puerto Rock from New York's Lower East Side. Six, "real" name Arthur, met Jee at Columbia University freshmen orientation three years ago, but he dropped out after his first semester. Six can't speak more than a few words of Spanish, but Boricua to the end, New York to the end, LES to the end.

It happened to Jee, or it happened to Terrell, a black kid from Brownsville, Brooklyn, who was Six's roommate in college. Terrell loves Brownsville but he doesn't believe in it. He believes in people and their ability to change, to be more than their upbringing, their block, their neighborhood. He believes in getting his family out of the 'Ville. Terrell thinks that he is living proof of his beliefs.

It's all real. Do believe me.

## WEDNESDAY

Lick lick, find the seam, lick lick lick. Be careful, the seam runs diagonal. Six'd rather just use a sponge or run it under the tap but skilling Dutches is something I enjoy and the effort I put into it, I get back, word up. Suck it up and down once for good measure. Crack off the rounded end, easier to peel an edge and pull the skin off that way. Real gentle, tug the skin off. This one's fresh, I hate stale-ass Dutches. Defeats the whole fucking purpose. Like the niggas who break Dutches down the middle. Fuck is the point of that? Gotta peel the skin and then crack the inner shell 'cause when you roll, the skin wraps tighter than just splitting the whole thing at once. You gotta skill a Dutch 'cause how you skill it, really take your time with it, affects how smooth the pull is, how many pulls you get, how even the weed is distributed, how the el feels rolling between the index and middle fingers, then index and thumb. What you put into it, you get back. Everything matters, you know?

Even smoking blunts. Smoking with Six, in his crib, it's strictly blunts. Preferably Backwoods, though they too sweet for me. No joints. *Fuck is that?* Six, would say. *White boys suck the white dick, niggas smoke the brown one.* Ghetto pride shit. Probably why he doesn't smoke pipes or bongs, either, too hippie for him. Terrell, on the other hand, that nigga'll smoke anything. Once he showed me how to smoke out an apple, some shit he learned from hanging out with too many crazy white college niggas. Now the skin is off, this is my special touch. Put the skin in a shallow plate with a little bit of Henny in it. Eases the tobacco taste and gives it a lil' something extra.

*Son, is that shit ready yet!?! You baking a cake nigga? Cono!*
*Relax kid, just skilling it.*

*Fuck skillin, start sparking son.* Six with a smile in the corner of his mouth.

*It's drying now kid, relax. Give it like five.*

*Throw that shit in the microwave Jee, ya heard?!*

*Patience Art, patience is a virtue.*

*Son, who the fuck was talking to you? You can't even hardly smoke anyway, Terrell. Turn into mutherfuckin Schnarf and shit. Remember that Thunder Cats shit? Schnarf, Schnarf. Petro ass nigga.* Still smiling.

*Whatever whatever.*

*Schnaaaarf, Schnaaaarf. And don't light that bogie in here, cigarettes is outside, ya heard? You know that Tio Tom, I mean, Schnarf, I mean, Terrell.*

T, always rising up when he's getting punked, even out of fun. Not usually to fight or anything but just to remind niggas of his size, that if you gave him a fair one, the nigga could knock you out, though I never seen it. Probably a habit from growing up in the 'Ville. T's too nice, too fucking reasonable to fight, but he really don't like being called Uncle Tom, even in Spanish. Not that he hasn't heard it before, but from black kids, not a Puerto Rock like Six. T's funny that way, like only black kids can call him Tom or say nigga.

*Oh you swelling up on me nigga? Sit your about-to-graduate-Columbia-University, nicotine-addicted ass down son.*

*Like you don't smoke Art. And watch all that nigga this and that coming out of your mouth.*

*Why don't you watch all that nigga shit for me, nig-gah.* Six, smiling from ear to keloid.

*Whatever. I'm going to the fire escape for a cigarette. Jee, let me know when that blunt's ready.*

*No doubt.*

Six, a bully nigga, always punking someone when he can. From clowning to drama in six seconds flat. Funny as hell, especially if you're his friend, but a bully. On the low, I'm glad T is here to deal with Six's shit. I used to catch it a lot, especially being Asian. Even though Six grew up with Chinese kids in his neighborhood and school, he never hung out with them too tough. So when we were first getting cool, he used to make all types of jokes. I'm used to it though, been hearing them all my life, growing up around black and Spanish kids not knowing who the fuck this Korean kid is. *Yo Jee, tell your moms to stop putting that cat in my shrimp fried rice, gook.* Catch shit, gotta snap right back. *Okay, only if your uncle the super can bring me some Goya beans after he fixes my sink, nigga.* Ghetto survival skills. Every new school, new neighborhood, new set of peoples, it's almost like I had to go through it to recognize that I was different, a new yellow face in a mix of brown and black, but not a punk. Not scared, stuck up, or stupid. Outsiders gotta be patient, nobody gives up their trust that quick.

Six though, that nigga just likes to break on people. I call it the sixth borough complex. See, Six grew up in the Lower East Side where Puerto Ricans, Chinese, and blacks live on top of one another, mad tight, but at least it used to stretch from Fourteenth and Second to the north and west (and in the summer up to Twenty-third, the Asser-Levy pool) all way down to Chinatown, as east as the river and as south as the Brooklyn Bridge. A little, distinct ghetto world smack in the middle of lower Manhattan. So LES niggas call it sixth borough, a world unto itself with a flavor like no other borough. Just like Harlem ain't Manhattan, it's Harlem World, LES is sixth borough.

That was the eighties, though, when LES was full of dope fiends and stick-up kids. Now, you got all the white shitheads—European and Israeli tourists, college students, art fucks, imported punk rockers—looking for cheap rent pushing in from the east and even the south, bumrushing Chinatown. Surrounded on all sides, crackers even renaming shit as far east as Avenue A, calling it East Village. Jacking rents on two-bedroom apts up to $1,800 and pushing LES niggas farther and farther east. Eventually into the East River, not giving a fuck if niggas drown or make the swim to cheaper housing in one of the other boroughs. I call these crackers pioneers, exploring the "uninhabited wild west," which is really just jerking the niggas that've been there the whole time. Just like all the other pioneers you hear about in high school history class. It's called gentrification, one of the few real things I've learned in college. Also known as white motherfuckers doing what they do best: shit on niggas, spics, and gooks.

Where we are right now, Lillian Wald Houses on the Av, is the last bit of land for cats like Six, squeezed in like a motherfucker. T calls it a Napoleon complex but to me, it's just sixth borough, a borough that's getting hemmed in on all sides, squeezed into just a couple blocks. Sixth borough complex, needing to wile out, lash out, fight back and shit. And that's why I call him Six, though his government name is Arthur.

Add to all that dropping outta Columbia 'cause of funds after only a semester, then having to move back into the PJs with his aunt made Six a kid with a short temper and an ill sense of humor. You just have to learn how to accept both and laugh. And that's what I do.

*T, Six, this shit is dry, y'all ready to spark?*
  *Been ready son. Spark it.*
  *Gather round the cipher, I got a story to tell.*

*Fuck, I think I lost my menthols, a new pack too of them expensive Nat Shermans you got me hooked on, Jee.*
  *At least they brown like you. Not some white-ass Newports. Like you always say, niggas smoke the brown dick.*
  *True indeed. Regardless, they gone. T, go to the store, nigga, I need a loosie and a Snicker bar, word uppp nigga.*
  *You go to the store man, it's your neighborhood. You Mumra-looking motherfucker. And I told you to relax with all the nigga this and that shit.*
  *Oh shit, Tom cursed! The nigga must be zooted!*
  *Whatever Art. And stop that nigga shit I said.*
  *What, you not my nigga, T? Jee ain't your nigga?*
  *I'm not saying that. We're all friends, but I don't like the calling each other nigga shit. I don't like hearing it coming out of your mouth.*
  *Listen Schnaaarf, we all niggas son. Even this gook-nigga Jee. We all seen the same shit, ya heard?*
  *Not the same shit.*

T and Six, old fucking roommates, best friends (or enemies) and shit when they get lit. I bet they had this conversation twenty times when they lived together. Shit don't ever die though, not while the world still exists. Not while niggas is still struggling, still niggas. I try to stay outta all that. I know some niggas get upset when I say it, since I'm Korean. So I try to keep it in my cipher, my peoples, my niggas. People who know where I'm coming from and I know where they're at. Nothing more than that. But even now, in my cipher, I don't say much. T gets real aggie and who the fuck am I to say anything anyway?

*Son, maybe you seen some shit I haven't or Jee hasn't, just on some black shit. But I seen some shit too as a Puerto Rock growing up in LES that I know you haven't.*

*First of all, LES whatever, I'm from Brownsville. And regardless, it's a term from my history, not yours or Jee's. It's my grandparents, parents, and me that have lived with that word for generations, not you.*

*You don't think I been called a nigga? Spic, nigga, all that shit! And Jee called a gook by some cracker motherfucker?*

*Yeah T, that's why I don't bug the fuck out when one of y'all calls me gook, as long as it's with love. Now it'd be a different story if some white kid who thought he was cool with me called me a gook. Then I'd flip. But one of y'all? Naw, to me, that's taking that shit back from the motherfuckers who put it on me. By the way, you know where that word came from?*

*Some Vietnam War shit.*

*Naw kid, the Korean War. After the Japanese got kicked out, the American GI fucks came to rule and Koreans thought they was gonna save them. So when they saw the GIs, they started yelling mi-gook, mi-gook, the Korean word for America. These racist ass soldiers thought they were calling themselves gooks, me gook, me gook, and called them gooks, even after they fucking learned what the shit meant. That shit stuck forever, the Vietnam War, all that shit, and now it's for all Asians and shit.*

*Well, whatever you want to do with gook, that's your decision. For me, nigga is my term, my decision to flip and use with whoever. Not every Asian feels like you, right Jee? And not everyone wants to even hear it, ever. And what if every white kid in Iowa started calling each other gook, like they do with nigga. It's not their term, their history to fuck with, it's yours right? Same thing with nigga, it's my history. And when that shit gets thrown around by any and everyone, my experience, my history gets lost.*

Damn, niggas T and Jee always getting on some academic history type shit. Six smiling, sarcastic.

*Anyways . . . T, I hear you completely on that kid. But that's why I'm talking about just speaking within our cipher, our people, not any motherfucker from anywhere, especially not a white kid, some cracker. And that's the reason why I have no fear of calling white kids crackers. You know where that shit comes from?*

*Yeah, slave masters cracking the whip. Slaves would call him their master a cracker.*

*Word. And it's like for me, I'll call any white kid a cracker so they don't forget they history, where they come from. Feel me?*

*But it wasn't Asian slaves Jee, they weren't your ancestors.*

*You don't think Asians were shitted on throughout this fucking country's history? You never heard of indentured labor back in the day? And to this day too?*

*Exacto! We all niggas here T. That's what I been trying to tell you son. Fuck all the history shit son. Today, right now, we all niggas. All niggas, son!*

*But I'm the only nigger here.*

*But to the white motherfuckers that run this country, we all niggas. Peep this son. It's like I told Jee the other day. Peep this shit: Niggas, Indigenous, Gooks, Arabs, and Spics. N, I, G, A, S.*

*We all niggas son. All niggas in the big picture of this fucking country.*

*That's clever and all Art, but the bottom line is that it's a word from my history, and not yours to decide.*

*Six, T, let's just dead this shit. We going in circles.*

*You think I ain't a part of your history nigga? I may be Puerto Rican, but look at my skin, my hair? This shit is not from laying out on the beach at Coney Island nigga. And anyway, whatever your history son, where you at now? A bitch nigga at Columbia. So Ivy League trained, nigga can't even curse.*

*That's by choice . . . and you were there too, Jee's still there.*

T's glued to his seat, Six is grilling him, and I'm sure the weed don't help. Nigga looks shook, for real. Damn T, shoulda dropped it. Now it's getting heated.

*AND, where you from, been, whatever. All I know is that we been in situations, tight situations where niggas know how to act and some niggas don't. Bootleg niggas like you. Bitch niggas. Jee's my nigga cause he comes through in the clutch. A real nigga and shit.*

*Like when Art? When have I not come through?*

Damn T, shoulda let it slide. Don't you wanna just enjoy the high? Damn kid, now we gotta bring up old shit.

*Come on nigga, you know there's a million stories like that. Like that time when we was all on Eleventh and B, remember Jee, this summer son, the sneaker store?*

*Yeah . . . but that was all that Korean shit with the kicks, oh shit, that shit was bananas. Banoodles son.*

*Straight platanos kid.*

*Straight yucca nigga!*

*Tuberous!!!*

22

*Ooooh shit, that nigga T said tuberous.*

Good, everyone laughing. No more fucking up our high. I hope.

*Fucking bitch college nigga. You forgot already Jee? That was the day T turned straight bitch! Nigga didn't even stick around, nigga got scared and shit! I don't even know why you laughing T, you weren't even there.*

*Fuck you Art. That's not what happened.*

*Both of y'all chill out.* Damn Six, you got your point across. And T, forgot already? Told you, shoulda let it slide.

I think it happened in May. It was the last time Chous had come up to New York and when I realized I might not be coming back to Columbia in the fall. "Academic probation" meant my financial aid was getting cut, a lot. I knew I had been slipping, smoking a little too much. I felt like wiling a little, being wreckless, before I had to sit down and figure out the details, what I would do, if I would go back to Philly or not, and hardest of all, how to tell my mom. So I started hanging out with Six a lot more and making a couple of missions to Philly every month, just to see if Chous had anything for me to get into. Sometimes I wouldn't even tell my mom I was in Philly, especially if Chous had a scam set up for us. Just troop it down there, hustle some laptops or weed or whatever Chous or his friend Walt was into, and then jet back with some loot. I wasn't g-ing off, building stacks of cash or anything, but it was enough to live on.

Around May, I'd just spent a week down in Philly with my moms and when I came back up, Chous came back to New

York with me to take care of some shit he and Walt were scheming. When he finished what he needed to, we decided to go out, burn a tree, hit a club downtown. So me, Chous, and T made a run down to LES to link with Six, cop a bag and get into something. T had no idea that Chous was carrying.

Six was dry, so we walked down to the spot on Eleventh to cop some boom but it was some bullshit.

*That was some schwack ass weed kid.*

*Jee, what the fuck is that, schwack?*

*That's my new shit Cinco, schwag and wack equals schwack.*

*That's five you dumb ass nigga. Try Seises, you non-Spanish speaking nigga. And anyway that must be some Philly shit. Chous, the fuck you bringing up from there and putting in Jee's head son?* Laughing at his own jokes, as usual.

*Chill nigga, that's his own shit. But hold up, check that out over there.*

I knew from the switch in Chous's voice, from loud and lighthearted to low and serious, that he was scheming. We looked up and saw a short, stocky-looking white kid approaching from down the block.

*You feel me, right Jee?*

*No question kid.*

Six put three and three together real quick . . . *I never seen him before.*

Meaning he wasn't local and could be run on without neighborhood drama. Probably just one of the East Villagers, a homesteader, a pioneer. Six was already up off the stoop and ready, always ready for a violator in his borough.

*You holding kid?*

*Yup,* Chous whispered.

24

*He looks like some Hell's Angels dude.*

Damn T, already thinking of ways to back us down.

*No he fucking don't. Son, don't even think about bitching on this Terrell.*

Chous whispered, *Y'all got me, right?* And stood up. The kid got closer, looked up, and then stepped quicker to get by us a little faster. Chous, no fear, even in unknown territory.

*You got the time man?*

The kid froze and just stood there. Diesel, thick-necked, crew-cut, tatted from neck to wrist. The Chinese character on his forearm and dragon wrapping from his elbow to his shoulder tensed, then calmed. By the time I looked up back at his face, Six had already maneuvered behind him.

Seven dollars, thirty seconds, and sixteen credit card digits later we decided he'd take us sneaker shopping. Actually, Chous decided it. I thought it was too risky but he was heated that the kid was broke and determined to make it worthwhile. By the time we got to the sneaker store on Fourteenth, T had jetted and we didn't even notice. Probably just walked away on the way to the store while we were focused on this white kid, Darren. I covered for him later, saying he couldn't afford any drama being so close to finishing school and whatnot. But I was vexed, too. Chous stared me down; T was my boy and there wasn't no fucking excuse. It took almost the whole summer for T to be able to show his face around Six. Chous didn't wanna see T ever. Loyalty, having each other's backs no matter what, was everything to Chous.

Six kept his hands in his pockets the whole time, even though he wasn't strapped, to help motivate Darren make the walk. But Chous's approach was to be friendly with Darren and talk to him. Before we walked in the store, Chous explained to Darren what was going to happen, like they were old friends, one doing the other a favor. We'd pick out shoes, he'd pay for them on his card, then we would leave and let him go. Darren spoke to Chous easy enough, like he wasn't being run on the whole time. Chous asked him all types of friendly questions. Darren told us he was a student at Cooper Union studying sculpture, originally from Florida. When he told us he just moved to Fourth between A and B, Six gave him some encouragement.

*Son, so we know where you live. We can come find you. Do remember that when we in the store.*

Good cop, bad cop shit. Chous on one side, Six on the other. It was almost funny.

Darren looked a little stiff as we stepped into the store, and I thought maybe he had shit his dirty, paint-stained overalls from his nervous, straight-legged walk. I kept thinking about him shitting himself. Something to make me chuckle and ease my own nerves. Especially when I saw that the store owner was Korean. He was walking in between the back and cash register. This was too close to home, but Six was like, *Naw son, you can skill this. It'll make it even easier. Just poly with the nigga in Korean and shit.*

The young Puerto Rican kids working in the store knew something was funny, and there was a couple times I looked over to Chous to see if he wanted to jet. But everyone was cool enough and we spent fifteen minutes trying on kicks. Chous even had Darren try on a pair of blue and yellow Asics, told him they looked good on him. But Darren said no thank you, he just wanted to buy our eight pairs of sneakers and leave. Chous

obliged and they walked up to the counter. I was glad I didn't
have to go up and do that shit.

I was looking at the shelves to see if there was any other colors to add to the two pairs of Air Maxes I picked and keep from
looking around and getting nervous when Six leaned over and
told me to go to the counter and see what was happening with
Chous and Darren. One of the employees had called the owner
from the back because of a problem with Darren's credit card.
The owner was an older Korean man, in his forties. An ah-guh-
shee. Chous had already started to get heated. I could tell
because I could hear broken-up Korean curses rising from a
mutter in his gut to venom in the top of his throat. Fuck.

*What's the problem kid?* His eyes were chinked, vexed.

*Jee, this ah-guh-shee sehk-hee mother . . . trying to tell me
that we over the card limit and shit. I told him we'd take a pair
out. Now he asking for another ID on top of the driver's license
we already gave him! Like he don't trust us and shit.*

*Yo relax, relax Chous.* This wasn't Chous. He didn't go off
so easy in Korean. One of the Korean traits his mom had managed to instill in him was a respect of elders, Korean elders at
least. Or maybe it was just the situation. Me and Chous
worked in my mom's sneaker store just like this one growing up
in Philly, until that summer in '90 when we got stuck up
together. And now it was the opposite; we were the niggas running the store for kicks. I didn't like thinking about the situation, and Chous didn't like being in it.

I looked up at the ah-guh-shee behind the counter. His jaw
was stiffening and his brow was getting dark. He was staring at
Chous, cornrowed, thick-lipped, light-skinned, passable for
Puerto Rican, Vietnamese, or light-skinned black, spitting half-

intelligible, broken Korean curses, revealing the chink in his eyes and quick Korean temper.

Collecting myself, I switched to good Korean immigrant mode, the one that got me into Columbia and let me put up with white people I needed shit from, and said in my most respectful Korean: *I'm sorry sir. I'm sorry for my friend too, he has no manners. My friend Darren has more ID, it's not a problem at all. And if we spent too much for the credit card, we can take some sneakers out. I'm very sorry.*

I surprised myself with my Korean. I was out of practice, but the situation made me spit it, without thinking, and it came out pretty good. Chous's face was like, Damn.

The two employees were staring. They probably thought at first that this was just another Korean kid coming in and getting a big discount or at least no tax, just for speaking a little Korean, the way that Koreans look out for each other: *These fucking gooks. I been here two years and the nigga still charges me tax. This gook just walks in, spits a few Korean words, and walks out with a big discount.* But they must've seen the situation was different. The owner too tense and the mix of races too random. Plus they recognized Six, knew the nigga's reputation. So they kept their distance, putting shoe boxes away while they kept an eye on us in case some shit happened.

The ah-guh-shee warned me loud enough for Chous to hear that he should watch his mouth. Chous understood what he said but couldn't unscrew his face, he was too heated. I asked him to step back and let me handle it.

*Go chill over with Six kid. Near the door yo. For real, I'll handle this. Trust me kid.*

Chous didn't know if he should be offended or not.

*Trust me, have my back on this kid. And tell Six to be easy too.* Chous slowly turned around and walked toward the door, where Six was standing, ready to jet.

In a real low voice, I explained to the ah-guh-shee that Chous was half black and that's why his Korean manners were so rough. I told him that I was a student at Columbia University and didn't mean to disrespect him in any way. Language that he could accept. The anger didn't fade from his face but his words were calmer.

I looked back and everyone—Chous, Six, the employees—looked confused. Almost as confused as Darren, who only snapped out of it when I barked at him to pull some other ID out. Took my nerves out on Darren, relaxed myself. I parleyed with the storeowner long enough with many many apologies to get the nerve to ask him if we could charge a gift certificate to the credit card to max it out, but he only offered a no-tax discount. I was about to turn it down, but realized it woulda looked real suspect and accepted it.

After a few more thank-yous, apologies, and a quick, deep bow, we left with Darren and walked him a few blocks away. He looked so confused that I wondered if he would even bother to call his credit card company. It took him a second to understand that he could go.

*Yo, bounce son! Fourth and A son, remember. We know where you fucking live. Now get the fuck out of here!*

Darren turned up the block at a brisk pace. I thought for a second he might go run to the police but figured, or hoped, him to be smarter than that.

I wasn't sure if Chous had heard everything I said in the store so I watched his face when he told Six about the gift certificate request. Chous was defensive about his Korean, but my stepping in and apologizing for his manners was the right move. And since I'm older, Chous's Korean hyung, a little punking was acceptable. But blaming his race was stepping over a line, even if it was just to calm the storeowner down. I felt bad and ready for anything; flipping on a friend and letting his temper come to blows was part of loyalty to Chous. But there wasn't any sign of anger, and they laughed the entire way back to Six's crib. I tried to relax but I kept hearing sirens. I think it was just somebody's high-pitched laugh or squeal in the distance. I didn't say a word and just smoked a cigarette. I felt dizzy, like I had just stepped off a roller coaster and spent all my energy squeezing the safety bar.

*Jee-Yong ah, your friends, our family is like bi-bim-bap. All different vegetables, meats, rice, hot sauce mixed in together like crazy.*

*What do you mean, ahm-ma?*

*Just look around. You and all your black and Puerto Rican friends. Your white girlfriend, Karen.*

*Karen's not my girlfriend, ahm-ma. I told you that before.*

*Anyway, and your sister's Filipino boyfriend. All mixed together, like bi-bim-bap.* My mom holds in a laugh, half funny, half embarrassment.

*Is there something wrong with that?*

*No, nothing wrong with it. It's just, what would your uncles and aunts and grandparents in Korea think?*

*Or even uncle out in Bluebell?*

*Mmnnnn.*

*But we didn't grow up in the suburbs, ahm-ma. We're here. My friends I grew up with, right here. Black, Puerto Rican, whatever.*

*Like Chous, whatever. Mixed together like bi-bim-bap, whatever style. Poor Chous, his Korean's so bad.*

*But better Chous than all the stuck-up white friends that my cousins have out in Bluebell. Cousins that only date white and whose Korean is even worse than Chous's.*

*That's true. And I think growing up like you did saved you from all the money-chasing of so many of these Korean kids nowadays. I feel so bad you had to grow up the way you did, without money, in this neighborhood, but I also feel thankful. Life isn't all about cars and nice clothes. Maxima, BMW, Armani. And you know that, thank God.*

*I know. And it's not about being as white as possible.*

*Ah-goo, Jee-Yong, always the white thing. So much hate.*

*Not hate, love. Love of who we are, my friends, our neighborhood. And hate of how this country tells us to hate ourselves, being Korean, each other. So we can be more white.*

*Jee-Yong, don't start again.*

*I'm just saying, there's nothing wrong with being bi-bim-bap.*

*I know, nothing wrong with bi-bim-bap.*

# NEARER, MY GOD,
# TO THEE

## John Gennari

### I

The thing we all noted and snickered about was how William pronounced the word "against"—not the flat, matter-of-fact "agenst" you hear all the time, but "agAInst" with a quivering singsong middle and an elastic crescendo. It drew attention to the word, gave it oratorical heft. We speculated on whether this was a black thing ("didn't Martin Luther King pronounce the word that way?"), or just an affectation meant to make us feel a little less cultured. Harvard was all about these kinds of performances, and William was all about Harvard.

William was a scion of the Washington, D.C., Afrostocracy, born and bred to the struggle for black freedom and excellence. He was defying his family by not following his father and two siblings into medicine, or failing that, in not aspiring to public renown as a politician or power lawyer. His desire to become a professor was class-appropriate, but his chosen field of anthropology puzzled his family, it not being obvious how the study of Yoruba religion would lead to high government appointments or a listing in the social register. William had internalized a family code that made success and superiority obligatory, yet his was an antiestablishment elitism. He was a pan-Africanist filled with romantic ardor for the motherland, and a post-SNCC activist whose rich baritone echoed through Harvard Yard in elegant indignation at the university's complicity in South African apartheid. He was himself a marvel of African aesthetics, an ebony Adonis whose every movement pulsed with grace and mastery. He wore his clothes beautifully. One day, he'd go Afro-Edwardian in an understated Savile Row cut, the next day, he'd go native in a flamboyantly colorful dashiki. Even sneakers and jeans looked special on him, because they were on *him*, the same way perfectly mundane words sounded special coming off his tongue.

We were all in awe of William—his elan and cocksureness; his extraordinary mind and insatiable curiosity; his penchant for always being the most compelling person in the room. "We" were defined not so much by whiteness (my girlfriend at the time was Puerto Rican), but by the fact of our being in the presence of a more powerful and charismatic force. Put William in any group—including his current colleagues on the Harvard faculty—and the rest of the group becomes this kind of "we." One time, during one of our many late-night bullshit sessions, one of us asked William if he believed in God. "I believe in many gods," he said with a chuckle and a Cheshire cat glint in his eye. "Sometimes I think I'm a god."

The other extraordinary talent in our group was Walter, now an M.D./Ph.D. operating at the Nobel-hopeful level, frequently testifying before Congress on thorny bioethics issues. Himself accustomed to being the commanding presence in the room, Walter often challenged William's dominion, asserting the canons of scientific method and Cartesian rationalism against William's heady brew of cultural relativism and mysticism:

*William:* Sometimes I think: "I'm a little tired of life, I'm going to try death for a while. See what that's like. Take its measure. Do an ethnography of death."
*Walter:* I'm sorry, but I've got to call you on *this* one.

It often felt like William was putting us on, toying with us. Like at graduation, when William asked Bob, a Jewish pre-med from Queens, to join him in wearing a khafia instead of mortarboard and tassel, in demonstration of sympathy for the Palestinians. Or when he said he was dying to visit Minnesota and feast his eyes on all the beautiful blonds that Tucker, a former Twin Cities hockey star, was always raving about. Or when he came to me with a used LP he'd just bought, some hideous fusion band in an uncut live concert jam: "I thought you'd like this," he said. "It's really hard to listen to, like your Coltrane records."

Usually William *was* putting us on, using his ironic humor—sometimes sweet, sometimes wicked—to gain the upper hand. But this was also his way of expressing his deeply earnest desire to turn the group into an intimate fraternity, a family. I think everyone in the group assumed that we were in this for life: We knew each other's secrets and desires; we knew how to hurt each other, and then how to reconcile; we had our jealousies; we had broken down the intricacies of our relation-

ships with our parents and siblings; we had staked out our positions on all the pressing issues. How could we not remain
enmeshed in one another's lives in the years to come? Yet
William insisted that we ritualize and memorialize our collec-
tive identity, codify the experiences that later would invoke
and enrich our nostalgia. Hence the senior year common diary,
the bound notebook in which William—more than the rest of
us combined—scribbled furiously and brilliantly. This was
William the anthropologist, creating and collecting the data of
the group. It was also William the sentimentalist, nurturing
the common bonds of our affection. And it was William the
egoist, stage managing us into the supporting cast of his
unfolding drama.

William couldn't help but stand out, and he wouldn't have
it any other way. But he also wanted desperately to be just one
of the guys. He was both a Race Man and the ultimate integra-
tionist: He didn't want to be left out of anything. He was both
proud of and a bit puzzled by my interest in jazz, and I was to
tell no one that he didn't particularly care for the music and
especially didn't get John Coltrane or Ornette Coleman: he
could fake it well enough to pass muster in black intellectual
circles. At our famous dance parties, he'd pogostick punk/new
wave style to the B-52's "Rock Lobster," then commandeer the
whole room into a Soul Train line for Sugar Hill Gang's
"Rapper's Delight," Bob Marley's "One Love," P-Funk's "One
Nation Under a Groove," or some nameless Brazilian samba.
He'd be first to the middle, enthralling everyone with moves
that we imagined coming straight from the steamy clubs of
Lagos, São Paulo, Kingston, Harlem, or southeast D.C., places

we knew about only because of William, scenes we could only imagine through William.

He, on the other hand, seemed to have imagined the whole of our lives, and the lives of everyone he came into contact with. No experience, no thought, no language could be closed off to him. In coming years he'd speak Italian to me (even though mine wasn't good enough to converse with him), Spanish to my Puerto Rican first wife (to go with the "Yo Soy Borinquen" sign on his front door), Yoruba to his Nigerian wife and her family, and Portuguese to his Brazilian friends. At my first wedding, in Puerto Rico, he caught everyone's attention by dancing a salacious merengue with the bride. At my second wedding, marking my marriage into a black Nashville family of a class level closer to William's than mine, he stole the show by writing and reciting a traditional English ballad wittily recounting the unfolding of our romance ("To him Cleopatra was she; her Marc Antony he'd surely be"). Lately he's taken up classical violin with his two children, and the three conduct public recitals at tony addresses around Cambridge. The only sphere of human activity from which William excludes himself is American sporting life—not athletics per se (he's a tremendous swimmer), but the ball sports, which I and many of my other male friends regard as the touchstone of our masculinity, and which he regards as silly and racially demeaning. Once, for kicks, we shot some hoops. When I told him that he was quite possibly the worst basketball player I'd ever seen, he beamed with satisfaction. Even in failure, William has a will to mastery.

I've thought hard about William's penchant for total inclusion and total mastery, and the effect that it has had on our friendship. It raises questions for me that I can't easily answer. When I admire William's Olympian self-possession, gift for one-upsmanship, and power to shape situations to his own ends, is it a case of my admiring William for challenging assumptions about how a black man should sound and act? If so, does that mean that I always see him first as black, and thereby consign him (and our relationship) to the very boundaries of race that a loving friendship should seek to transcend? Conversely, when I resent or am made uncomfortable by his seeming lack of humility, is this a case of my tapping into the white man's age-old anxiety about "uppity" Negroes? Since we're both the products of elite educations and have both chosen to make our careers in academe, at what point might William's higher standing in the profession invoke my envy and threaten my abiding brotherly love for him, and what if anything would this have to do with race?

A few years ago, I was teaching at a university in central Pennsylvania, and William came to a nearby college to give a lecture. After the lecture, one of the student sponsors took us to a hotel bar, probably thinking this was the only place in town where a well-dressed, sophisticated black man could feel comfortable. After a cocktail or two, William suggested we find a place with more local color. We ended up in a scruffy hole-in-the-wall full of beer-guzzling students and locals, all men, many of them watching *Monday Night Football* on the tube. If there's anything William despises more than beer, it's football—not just the game, but the culture of boisterous, knuckleheaded masculinity that goes with it. And yet here he was ordering up pitchers of Bud and yelling "fuckin' a" in his best yahoo voice to a group of Eagles fans one table over. See, he seemed to say to these men whose interests and passions were so different from his: I can do this, too, if I so choose, and with more zeal than you. He seemed oblivious to the possibility that his performance might incite a bar brawl.

Then, too, there have been times I would've expected William to push for control of the scene and the moment, and instead, in modest displays of generosity crucial to the health of the friendship, he's ceded ground. One moment stands out in my memory. It was at my parents' house, an encounter involving my mother's brother Abbey, who William knew to be a legendary figure in my family. Abbey—who died a few years after this event—was a man of Tony Soprano–like physicality who ran a construction company in northern New Jersey with his older brother Joe. Abbey was the kind of guy who showed his affection by wrapping you in a headlock and squeezing you within an inch of your life. His highest praise for another man was to say that he was "strong as a bull"—something he said often about his own father, and also about my father, as if to confirm that my mother had chosen a spouse who passed muster with the men of the family. He said it about boxers (Rocky Marciano, Joe Louis) and other athletes who captured his fancy. He was also a man of deep romance and sentimentality: He died, the doctors said, of an enlarged heart, a fitting and poetic diagnosis, I thought, because that's the way he lived—with too much heart. He was infinitely gregarious and an inveterate ham performer. He used to buy records with the vocal track cut out so he could sing over the top of the band, in a kind of home-friendly version of karaoke. He was a Sinatra fanatic—he built one of Sinatra's mother's retirement homes—but his husky, glandular voice made the performance more effective when he imitated King Pleasure ("There I go/There I go/There I go/Therrrrre I go . . ."), Barry White ("Girl, I don't know, I don't know, I don't know why/ I can't get enough of your love babe"), or other of the thick-waisted, black mack-daddy singers he favored. I had told William all about Uncle Abbey's performances. It was my way of explaining something about my family's soulfulness.

On this occasion, William and his fiancée, Adama—a highly accomplished, majestic woman who had quit her post as protocol officer for the Nigerian president to make a life with William in the U.S.—were on hand as Abbey was holding forth with hunting stories. These were stories that my family had heard many times: stories about my uncles and my grandfather and other Italian men, hardworking laborers who loved the woods and open land that their hunting trips took them to, loved one another's company, and loved a good venison or rabbit stew. As we noshed on salami and cheese and roasted peppers, and as Abbey described a deer shooting in grisly detail, a distressed Adama suddenly interjected: "Uncle Abbey, I just don't understand how you can look into the eyes of an innocent animal and then shoot it." Abbey replied without missing a beat: "Honey, I'd shoot Bambi and Bambi's mother on Easter morning." Everyone except William and Adama laughed. My laugh was just enthusiastic enough to join my family in the joke, but tentative enough so that William and Adama hopefully could see that I was sympathetic to their puzzlement about what passes for humor in my family. William kept silent, giving Uncle Abbey the moment, and leaving me to work out my allegiances.

I I

The Pennsylvania school where William came to give that lecture a few years back is part of the state college system (it was known earlier as a "teachers' college"), a rung below the state university system, several rungs below the elite private schools. The student sponsor who shepherded us around the town's night spots was a bright working-class, biracial young man from Philadelphia. He told us that he was the first in his family to go to college, and that he liked being at a school where this was common because he could feel solidarity with his fellow students. William asked him if he had ever considered applying to an Ivy League school. He laughed and said no, he never saw himself in those terms, and besides, his financially strapped family couldn't afford it. William, clearly startled by the answer, asked him whether he knew that Ivy League schools had lots of money and gave big scholarships to needy students. The young man clarified: He knew he wouldn't feel comfortable at one of those schools and, really, it just wasn't something he'd ever considered. William was incredulous: Didn't his parents push him toward the Ivy League, or at least one of the elite liberal arts colleges? No, the student laughed, they just wanted him to go to college; any college would do.

At the time, I had my Harvard degree, my Ph.D. from the University of Pennsylvania, and two years earlier, with William's help, I'd been selected to be a visiting fellow at Harvard's W. E. B. Du Bois Institute, which made William and me colleagues at the nation's most prestigious institution for African-American studies. And yet, in some crucial respects, I still had much more in common with this Pennsylvania state college bootstrapper. Like him, I'd been the first in my working-class family to graduate from high school. My father grew up on a farm in northern Italy, immigrated after World War II to the Berkshires of western Massachusetts (where family forebears earlier had toiled in the bootlegging and speakeasy trade), and settled into a career as a welder of power transformers at the General Electric facility in Pittsfield. He was a lunch-bucket union man who put in close to forty years, sacrificing his hearing to the deafening roar of the factory floor. My mother grew up in an Italian neighborhood in New Jersey, just over the George Washington Bridge from New York. Like many Italian girls of her generation, she left school as an adolescent to work in the needlework trade, using the sewing skills she had learned from her mother. Through my youth, she worked in our basement on custom-made drapery and clothing alterations.

What distinguished me from the Philadelphia kid, and moved me closer to William even before I met him, was that I had grown up surrounded by people with more money and education than my parents and relatives. By the time I was born, my parents had quit the blue-collar ethnic enclave of Pittsfield for the more prosperous Berkshire town of Lenox, once known as the "inland Newport" because of the Gilded Age tycoons who built magnificent mansions ("cottages," they called them) against the backdrop of the town's lush rolling hills. The only Italians in town were the descendants of the stonemasons, landscapers, cooks, and other tradespeople who had built and serviced the estate properties. My father and his brothers, whom he had helped bring over from Italy and set up in construction, built the house in which I was raised, in a neighborhood otherwise dominated by lawyers, doctors, and businessmen. Because of my parents' amiability, generosity, and live-and-let-live ethos, we became very friendly with most of them, including the family that lived behind us: a Swiss-born, antiunion General Electric executive and his Yankee Republican wife, who claimed *Mayflower* ancestry and who was astonished to discover that my parents spoke English.

Lenox and the surrounding area had been a mecca of nineteenth-century American literature and culture, home to Nathaniel Hawthorne, Herman Melville, Daniel Chester French, and Edith Wharton. After World War II, some of the former estate properties became venues of cultural tourism, most famously Tanglewood, summer home of the Boston Symphony Orchestra. Other properties became private boarding schools and upscale inns, resorts, and summer camps where many of us Lenox working-class and lower-middle-class kids washed dishes, waited tables, caddied, parked cars, and cut grass. To lubricate relations with the locals who both profited from and resented the influx of the summer people, the BSO allowed area public schools to hold their graduation ceremonies at Tanglewood. There, on a lovely June night in 1978, my parents wept with pride—and everyone else yawned and fidgeted—as I delivered my valedictorian speech and collected enough scholarship money so that the house wouldn't have to be remortgaged in order for me to go Ivy.

I was the first from my high school to go to Harvard for as long as anyone could remember, but I just as easily could have ended up at a completely different kind of place. As a junior, in fact, I had pursued a commission to West Point. Watching the

Army-Navy football game on television, I learned that the military academies paid for your education in return for five years of service, which seemed a fine way to spare my parents an expense they clearly wouldn't be able to handle. Luckily, a new humanities teacher at my high school, a true Renaissance man who inspired my interest in the world of art and ideas (and who paid the price in having to read my 120-page term paper on Dostoyevsky and Solzhenitsyn), steered me away from the military and encouraged me to think of myself as a writer.

I had always loved language, the sound of language as much as the written word. I was a child of the golden age of television, my ear conditioned by the brisk repartee of *The Beverly Hillbillies* and the slick double-entendre of *Batman*. While my parents read the local newspaper and an occasional magazine, I never saw them reading a book, and they didn't read children's stories to me or my younger brother and sister. As in many Italian-American working-class households, privacy was hard to come by, and loud voices constantly ricocheted off the walls, conditions that made for a loving family life but worked against a reading habit. "Shut up, Johnny's trying to read!" my mother would yell, adding another layer to the cacophony of television, radio, sewing machine, electric mixer, and boisterous relatives.

I was offered a scholarship to a journalism school after winning a competition that asked for an essay on the significance of the ERA. Knowing nothing about the women's liberation movement but a great deal about baseball, I crafted an argument about the shortcomings of the earned run average as a statistical measurement of pitching proficiency. The other possibility that loomed up after I turned down the West Point commission was an athletic scholarship. I was a three-sport letterman and a good enough hockey player to attract the interest of recruiters. My first college acceptance came from Holy Cross, whose hockey coach had come to visit our home. When the acceptance letter came, my parents were ecstatic—Johnny is going to college! The other acceptance letters that followed from Williams and Harvard—where my teacher/savior had encouraged me to apply, going over the head of the school guidance counselor, who told me those applications were wasted money—elicited far less impassioned responses. The prestige differences between these institutions didn't register: College was college. It meant that I'd have a shot at a white-collar life that might be easier on the back and the joints.

But would it be a better life? Would I sleep better, laugh more, dance more? Certainly I never would eat any better than I did at home, where my father's garden yielded a full year's harvest of magnificent vegetables, and my mother knocked out nightly meals that rich Americans could find only in gourmet Italian restaurants—the pastas, risottos, and polenta-based stews that my peasant ancestors invented to stave off starvation. When my parents dropped me off in Cambridge, their pressing concerns were these: Where would I eat? What if I got hungry when the dining hall was closed? What if I needed some shirts ironed? When the graduate student RA—a regal Turkish fellow, a doctoral student in government and an Olympic middle-distance runner—came by to introduce himself, my father's one question for him was this: What time is curfew here? "If he gets in any trouble," my dad conspiratorially whispered to him, "you just give me a call."

I was only mildly embarrassed by my parents' first interaction with official Harvard, no more than by the name tags that my mother sewed into my underwear so she could lose less sleep worrying about my doing my own laundry in a public facility. Then and later—such as at my graduation, when my mother, hearing that Walter's father knew how to jitterbug, grabbed him for a few twirls around the dais, undeterred by the absence of music and the ongoing diploma ceremony—I was humored, and I was proud. I was proud of my parents' utter lack of self-consciousness in this setting, their tacit confidence in their own way of life and their own values. Above all, I valued their sense of the home—not just the family, but the home—as emotional core, the garden and the refrigerator as indispensable safeguards of body and spirit. I knew there was more to life—that there were good and true things in this world beyond my refrigerator-of-origin—and my mother did her best not to saddle me with guilt for leaving the family nest. This required something of a heroic battle with her strongest instinct, a maternal feeling as strong as my father's hands and back. Leaving home for many Italian men is tantamount to a kind of social death, and when I left for college, my mother and sister sobbed hysterically as I've only seen them do at funerals.

Before leaving home, I thought that dinner-table conversation among college-educated people was all about literature, philosophy, and politics—not, as in my home, about last night's dinner, tomorrow night's dinner, the relative merits of Asiago and Parmigiano-Reggiano cheese, and the great time everyone had picking wild mushrooms up on the mountain with Uncle Tulio. I've long since learned that even English professors don't talk Shakespeare and Joyce with their children, and I've grown to cherish the sound of my family as an aesthetic experience akin to listening to one of Charles Mingus's joyous cacophonies. Still, I craved and grew to love and define myself by the cool, measured intellectual discourse of my college buddies. We talked women and we talked music—and then we kept talking. We talked Marx, Freud, Durkheim's theory of suicide, Weber's theory of rationality, Einstein's theory of relativity, laissez-faire economics, African pantheism, colonialism, Cubism, communism . . . hell, all the isms, and all the ologies too. This, too, became home.

William knew the most and articulated his ideas the most eloquently, but he also knew how to lay back and let the colloquy come to him. This wasn't hard for him to do because each of us, in his own way, was performing for him, the same way we'd perform for the teachers we had targeted as mentors. William encouraged the dynamic by feigning ignorance, flattering our intelligence, making us feel that our insights were absolutely crucial to his understanding of the world—all by way of feeding his mastery of the scene. I remember William saying that he was learning more from me than from his professors; that our friendship was the most valuable thing he was getting from Harvard. He had a way of approaching every exchange, every idea, every expressive act as if it were about him, aimed at him, conceived for his benefit or his harm. He imagined himself as the Archimedean point around which everything revolved. He never asked how he fit into the scheme, but instead what the scheme could do for him.

I might have felt patronized by William if I weren't so busy learning from him how to navigate the world of the social and intellectual elite. William looked more like the face of "diversity," but I was the true beneficiary of Harvard's affirmative action policy. He had been groomed for this experience since he left his mother's womb; I was an experiment in the liberal scheme to loosen up the class order. We were both outsiders to the WASP establishment, but we were both experienced in demystifying that establishment from the vantage of our class positions. My experience was that of a servant—I continued to work as a waiter, bartender, and caterer through college and graduate school—who peers inside the lives of the rich while mixing their drinks. William's experience was that of a member of a parallel establishment—the Afrostocracy—that exhibits many of the same characteristics of the WASP establishment and sometimes intersects with it. His having attended an elite Washington, D.C., prep school, for instance, meant that William came to Harvard already hooked up with a group of rich white friends, and keen on finding more. As a member of the servant class, I had spent plenty of time in the company of the *parents* of rich white kids my age, but very little time with those kids, since most of them were off in boarding school. William often told me how astonished he was at how nicely rich white people, especially really rich white people, treated him. I couldn't say the same.

One advantage of being William's friend is that he has excellent taste in rich white people. Through him, I was able to target the most thoughtful, interesting, socially conscious of the tribe, and not waste my time on the second-raters. Harvard at this time was full of rich white kids who were into reggae— the trustifarians, I liked to call them. If you walked into a party and heard Bob Marley, what you were sure to find was a sweaty mass of slumming preppies dancing in a uniquely arrhythmic, kinesthetically challenged style. From deep in the haze of weed smoke, William would emerge with the white guy who was applying for a fellowship to do ethnographic work on gender dynamics in Jamaican dance halls.

As fascinating and friendly as these rich-white-friends-of-William turned out to be, none was as interestingly self-reflexive as William was. They may have been doing good things with the resources at their disposal, and their self-consciousness about their class privilege may even have driven them to do truly progressive things, but they weren't interested in subjecting themselves—their breeding and their breed—to rigorous examination. They weren't, that is, anthropologists of their own experience. This William and I most emphatically were, and this is the ground on which we've forged much of the substance of our friendship.

As young academics, we think in terms of research projects, and it was William's hope that, once I finished with my jazz book, I might next use my American studies training to tackle the Washington, D.C., black bourgeoisie. I'd have plenty of material to work with, and not just from my friendship with William. I've had other close relationships in that world, and with the exception of one romantic partner, they've all had the same urge to embrace me as a curio—a white person without money—and nurture me as a privileged insider. It was William who gave me entree, starting with an invitation to a family wedding—his older sister's marriage to another of D.C.'s best-and-brightest—that deserved its own section in the social pages. The ceremony, at the National Cathedral, came with a multiple-page program complete with family genealogies and curriculum vitae detailing the couple's high achievements in medicine and the law. It was an event rich with possibility for a scholar interested in kinship networking and the forging of cultural capital.

But, alas, the scholarly urge dissipates when you're around people who show you love, even if they can't quite make sense of you. It doesn't help if you're a bit in awe of your ostensible subjects. In the days leading up to the wedding, as William and I ran errands and flirted with the bridesmaids, I couldn't help but notice that William's mother wasn't doing any cooking—an unthinkable thing in my house. But after a long and memorable talk with her about her role in Washington, D.C., civil rights organizing and local politics, I realized— maybe for the first time—that there's more than one way to nurture your children. On the day of the wedding, my assign- ment was to guard the entrance to the reception hall, letting in the five hundred some-odd invitees, keeping out the—as it happened—fifty some-odd people who showed up because they thought they should've been invited. How fitting, I thought. For what am I better cut out to do, by breeding and by inclination, than to throw around some muscle on behalf of the black bourgeoisie?

## III

During one of his early academic postings in a small New England town—just a few miles from where I grew up— William faced the same hassle that bedevils every black person brave enough to undertake an errand in the lily white wilder- ness: where to get a haircut. The idea of having to travel to the nearest city for this basic service struck him as not just unfair, but indicative of the college's cloudy understanding of what it means to live in a truly integrated community. And so William presented himself to a perplexed and resistant local barber, at once defiantly insisting on this merchant's obligation to serve the entire local public, and generously offering his own nappy head to the cause of uniracial hairstyling. Doing nothing to conceal his discomfort with having to finger a black scalp, the barber crudely jostled William's head and made a hash of the haircut. William could only read the treatment as racist, as he forcefully detailed in letters to the college president and the local newspaper.

One of the challenges of being the white friend of so righteous a black person as William is that it implores you to think harder about the burden of race, to recognize the unfairness of a situation in which black people not only have to deal with racism in ways you hadn't recognized, but then also end up having to take responsibility for educating people out of their ignorance. Truth be told, I was one of those people—call us liberals—who would think it was just great that this college was recruiting young black scholars, without fully considering what it would mean for a black person actually to live in such a community. At some point that black person needs a haircut. If that person is William, this becomes the occasion for exposing the community's de facto separate-but-unequal system, and for shaming both the practitioners of the system and those who support it through their ignorance and silence.

More truth be told, I wondered what in the hell possessed William to put himself at the mercy of a man wielding a razor and who knows what level of pent-up animus toward black people. However justified William's demand that this barber cut his hair, I wondered, frankly, if William's real motive wasn't a kind of vengefulness, a pleasure in the barber's discomfort, a pleasure so deliciously fiendish as to be worth the cost of a really lousy haircut—no small cost given William's vanity. Of course, if the problem that William was addressing is ever to be fully and fairly addressed, that barber *should* feel discomfort, at least as much discomfort as William felt in being rebuffed by him. But then why did *I* feel discomfort—to be more specific, why was I uncomfortable about the barber's discomfort? It certainly wasn't because I shared his revulsion for dark skin. No, there was something about the *power* that William exercised over him that unsettled me.

When I discussed this event with my wife, who I know never would put herself in the position that William did— she's never afraid of making white people uncomfortable if they deserve it, but she would never, *ever* let anybody mess up her hair—I was a bit surprised by the intensity of her response. "Thank you, William," she enthused, and then explained: "Don't you understand? In a way, William did what he did for *all* of us. Especially those of us who wouldn't have the guts to do it." Agreed, but not what I was looking for to resolve my ambivalent response to William's act, and no comfort at all as I reckoned with the way my whiteness seemed to be separating me from my wife and my friend.

Then she put a different spin on the case. "It's also about class. In a situation like that, for black people, money is power." Hearing this sparked memories of conversations with William, going back to college, when he'd talk about how important it was for him to dress well, the pleasure he took in shopping in the best places, how much he was looking forward to the day when he'd take his children to Saks and other upscale stores to outfit them for school. This was central to his vision of what it meant to be a good parent. I remember saying that I was all for nice clothes—still am—but that my vision of good parenting ran instead to the home-cooked family dinner—ideally, as in my parents' home, every night at the same time, to foster both the discipline and the pleasure of routine—and to teaching my son or daughter how to catch and hit a baseball.

But the class issue cuts even deeper, all the way to the bone. I realized, talking to my wife, that part of what explained my ambivalence about the barbershop episode was my identification with the barber as someone from the same world as my parents. I couldn't imagine my father, as a barber, subjecting William to the same racist treatment, and I know that if I told my parents about the incident, they'd understand William's position. I know, on the other hand, that I *could* imagine—and in fact have imagined—William wielding a kind of power over my parents, say by mimicking my father's habitual use of the word "ain't" or some other of my parents' working-class mannerisms, in a send-up along the lines of his performance that night in the hick bar in Pennsylvania. I also know that William has had a harder time than my white college friends feeling my parents' love, even as I know the love is there. I'd like to think this is because of class tensions, and not because of race. But I'm not sure. My other Harvard buddy Walter, the big-shot doctor and scientist, is in his own fashion—a fashion much more like my own—every bit as much an elitist as William. But unlike William, he comes off to my parents as "down-to-earth." Is this because he really is more down-to-earth, or because his whiteness enables him to appear as such to them?

A few years ago, when I got engaged to my wife, William said to me: "I just know that you're marrying a black woman so that you can get even closer to me." At first I thought this was another case of William assuming, godlike, that everything had to be about *him*. But on further reflection, I realized that so much of my life, as it has taken shape since I left home for college, *has* been about him. He is so much a part of who I have become—in how I talk and think and live in the world—that to resist or resent him is to deny a part of myself. The cost of embracing that new self is a certain critical distance from the world I grew up in and continue to love so much. So be it. An important friendship is priceless but not free.

# SOME
# WHITE MEN

## Elizabeth Alexander

My sophomore year in college, at the last moment one could sign up for classes, I came across the overlong, wildly ambitious syllabus for "Problems in the Study of African-American Literature" taught by the late Professor Michael Cooke. I had never taken a course in black anything before, never had a black professor, and did not suspect that I was on the cusp of transformation. I would ever after teach the literature I was about to read, become a writer, and explore and define myself and my place in the world with the help of those glorious books. The classroom had always been sacred space for me, a space where in some ways I felt most expansively myself as I attempted to articulate what I saw and felt in the books that were so precious to me. But that self had gone underground in my first year and a half at the university, and African-American literature was going to begin to bring it back into the light.

This was in the early 1980s, an era in which black feminism had made its mark and black feminist writers such as Audre

Lorde, Alice Walker, Barbara Smith, Toni Morrison, and Toni Cade Bambara made it clear to us women of color that we had to uphold our legacy, fight for our voices to be heard, defend the name of black women, tell the stories that had not been told, and in the words of the great Gwendolyn Brooks, "civilize a space/wherein to play your violin with grace." The authors favored in the English department at my university, where I was told that "nothing worth reading was written after 1600," were not yet called "dead white males"; it was a few years before the invention of that sardonic moniker, when the serious trench work of literary reclamation was well under way and when black literature as a field was still earning the respect that would allow it to exist. My small cohort fancied ourselves race and gender crusaders, putting out fires wherever we saw them, telling our stories for the first time, and basking in the afterglow of the blood, sweat, and tears shed on campuses by a previous generation. Each new book and conversation felt urgent and alive. Between feminism and "Afro-American" studies, it was all about being black girls together for my community and me, about working hard enough to live up to the standards of those fierce, tenacious women who had so brilliantly paved a way. Our idealized idea of mentorship involved naming and claiming the mothers and grandmothers and aunties, truth tellers of the kitchen table, organic theorizers, and survivors. In many of our relationships during those years with white women, peers and elders, we bumped up against the limitations of sisterhood and felt the sting of freshly identified and articulated gaps in understanding. We looked to the few black male faculty members for support and ate up their intelligence. Smart black men talking about black books and black people! Learning from them was an event unto itself. We were not yet consciously constrained by the role of the female student as dutiful daughter, and while we asked questions like, Why was there only one black female professor at the university? Why don't we read any women writers in our African literature class?, our bellies were full on learning and glorious blackness.

Mentorship was a kind of friendship, and the classroom was an intimate space. "Intimate" comes from the Latin *intimare*, to make known, from *intimus*: innermost. To be truly seen and known is arguably what we all wish for; to desire it in an intellectual context, in a community of learning, has particularly high stakes for black people, as we have been historically imagined and wrought as lacking any significant inner life, all surface yet presumed scrutable. Recall Thomas Jefferson's famous words from "Notes on the State of Virginia," words that I first learned in college and that became part of the elaborate intellectual coat of armor I wear to this day: "No black is capable of utterance above the level of plain narration." Those words teach us, Know thine enemy, but more importantly, Know thine history, and know what is at stake as you learn.

So if the classroom is a space where the life of the mind is developed and exposed, made visible as it is challenged and fortified, then to be a young person validated in that space constitutes what I contend is a certain kind of friendship. The mind is a life force to be respected and tended. To be etymological again, the word "friend" derives from a prehistoric Germanic word meaning "to love." Tending the mind of a student or younger person is love of a high order.

Now that I have been teaching long enough to have mentored many young people, I understand something about the pleasure my own mentors must have taken in me. The ego is involved, of course, in the same way that it is when we first fall in love. The student thinks the teacher's ideas are fascinating and brand new; the student's responses are also new to the teacher, and make her think about her own long-cherished ideas and the journey to articulate them. Sometimes a student's excitement takes the teacher back to those years in herself, that feeling like no other of reading a book that changes the way we think, see, feel. I've realized over time that I truly believe what I read in great books, or see in great paintings, or hear in great music. So how could I not profess gratitude to the teachers who have illuminated so much for me? When I have mentored a student particularly well—shepherded him or her through the job market vagaries, helped coax a poem to a new place, taught a book that rocked the student's world, I am often deeply self-satisfied, beyond the rewards for the student. Enacting one's articulateness, sharing one's knowledge, are some of what shines at the end of the tunnel of years of often isolated study and struggle. Our teachers make the young feel shiny because they are; the young burnish their elders and restore their luster, as though they are able to see it with special vision.

So what is there to say about white men and mentorship in looking back at one black feminist's beginnings in the era of searching for our mother's gardens? There is much to be said about what we work and write against, as June Jordan does so powerfully in her essay about being an undergraduate at the University of Chicago and encountering a white male professor who pronounced her writing "impenetrable to a rational reader," asked her if English was her first language, and made it clear that he thought she would never, could never, be a writer. I took a writing class in college with one nightmare teacher who fulfilled most negative stereotypes of how said beast should behave, expecting "ghetto authenticity" in my writing and refusing to distinguish me or my words from the other black girl in that very small class.

Or further back, I could talk about the white boys in high school—a small school with presumptions of felicitous community and widespread excellence—who said I "took their place" in the Ivy League with, they presumed, lower SAT scores. Or the teachers we were entrusted with, who were supposed to know so much more than we did, who never showed us one word written by a black person. Further along, there were the graduate oral examiners in the mid-1980s who referred to Ralph Ellison as a "Negro" and Harriet Jacobs's *Incidents in the Life of a Slave Girl* as "a story about some black girl stuck up in the attic." Then there were the ignorant faculty colleagues, white men who would say things in the name of presumptive colleagiality such as, "Of course we'd like to admit more black graduate students if they could just be more like you." All of these violations took place in what was supposed to be intellectual *community*. Then there are of course all the white men who intellectually disparage, refuse to hire, pay less, sexually fetishize, lie, hoard, steal, do not step up to the plate, the white men who manufacture and perpetuate so many of the human issues that have in part given black women something to write about and struggle against. I could go on.

I am not talking about those white men.

No, this is a moment in the tradition of the roll call and

shout out, to talk about another kind of white man. I want to talk about some white men who loved and nurtured and supported me as I came of age, and who took me seriously, thus taking seriously their own roles as elders in a human community. I begin with my cherished Uncle Herbie, my father's law school roommate and my godfather, a white, Jewish New Yorker who has always lavished me with the pure sunshine of his adoration and respect. Do we talk about "race," as such, or racial issues, or gender issues, or who we are vis-à-vis each other? No. That is not the nature of this relationship. He now tells me about what I was like as a child, why it's good to marry someone from a big family, why enormous, shameful mistakes are necessary in life, and, my favorite topic, what my parents were like as the twenty-somethings he met almost fifty years ago. Of course, all those years ago, race was an issue that the two friends could not have escaped. Just a few years before they met, for example, my father's college—Harvard, supposed pinnacle of enlightened American education—forbade black and white students from sharing dorm rooms. But whatever the two might have wrangled with over their long friendship, to Herbie, I was his child, which meant that the covenant of my tending was sacred.

Then there was my parents' friend Bill, who, in our living room and his, engaged me in Socratic dialogues about the issues of the day: school vouchers (then called "tuition tax credits"); self-determination for Washington, D.C., where I grew up; the morality (or immorality) and viability (or impracticality) of draft registration; etcetera. He probably took my intellect more seriously than any other person I knew in those years. We would argue hard; he cut me no slack; there was no hiding place in those exchanges, only toughness, endurance, and the sharp high notes of exhilaration at a debate well argued. He came from the Pacific Northwest and did not know a single black person (or Jewish person, for that matter) when he was growing up. He was no doubt exposed to ideas about black people, but whatever the case, what was important to him was that I was the child of his friends and that he liked the way I thought—he saw that I thought—and loved helping me do it better.

In college, there were two teachers in particular who, in the most unsentimental ways, made what we might now call a "safe space" for my thinking and writing voice to emerge and begin to sing. The poet Sterling Brown says, "every 'I' is a dramatic 'I,' " as a reminder that so-called creative writing is not necessarily autobiographical. But strong writing does come from some surprising place deep within that can catch writers themselves unawares, hence the idea that writing classrooms must be, to bend the current phrase, "safer spaces" than others. Students in nonwriting classrooms rarely share their work with one another (though it can be very fruitful to do so). At least some of the shields between us are let down when this barrier is broken. And though the "I" may need to be dramatic to succeed, first-person writing nonetheless makes us feel we are getting an intimate glimpse into a writer. That is part of its job.

So when a student in Mr. B.'s writing class used racial stereotypes to characterize a black male character in a story we read as a class, I remember how enraged and alone I felt as I tried to articulate, to the increasing resistance of the student and indeed much of the class, why the offending adjectives offended and, in fact, told us nothing that helped the story. Quietly, economically, simply, forcefully, Professor B. took my side, which is to say, he taught, and showed the way to what was indisputably, in this instance, right. His class was a writing class with its presumed intimacies; the student's racial stereotyping felt like a caustic betrayal of that closeness. Professor B.'s quiet, effective righteousness made that classroom a more deeply serious place where justice was present and palpable, and I imagine that many of the white students in the class understood the power of his example as well.

When I took the last class John Hersey taught, in the spring of my senior year, I had read enough of his work such as *Hiroshima* and *The Algiers Motel Incident* to know that he was interested in some of the kinds of issues—race as it intersects with violence and justice—that interested me. I also knew his writing was clean and cool, the quintessence of show-don't-tell. I was at that point a Black Woman Writer-to-Be, interested in exploring styles that could best be described as lush and lyrical in ascending increments. Metaphor was always present and always, infinitely, extended in my work. I wrote about places I had never been in the American South and Spanish-speaking Caribbean. My protagonists (all many shades browner than I and heart-stoppingly beautiful) lay with island men who ran with horses or city men who talked liberation politics and walked with an urgent swagger. Class rose to the surface of those stories like scum on boiled milk. My educationally privileged black heroines earnestly and awkwardly strove to "understand people who didn't grow up the same way she did"; other heroines held forth in glittering vernacular and commanded the streets to the clang and tinkle of their bangles and cowrie shell earrings. These were less plausible versions of the women I read about in those books that I so loved and watched at a distance on the streets of Washington, D.C., and New York City. I believed there was such a thing as a black and female voice, and I was trying to find and articulate it. In short, I imagined I was the anti–John Hersey, and though I respected his writing utterly, I thought, How will this man, this white man, this white man who writes so differently from me, make me a better Black Woman Writer?

That was before I met John Hersey—lucid, sturdy, steady, subtle, kind—and met in him someone who would see me clear as day, hear my voice and make it better, point me toward finding my own clarity. It was John Hersey who exposed my classmates and me to the first fiction of Jamaica Kincaid, her singular story "Girl": a strange, lyrical, arresting, black female Caribbean voice that showed me how many ways there were to tell a story. She didn't sound like any other writer I knew, and she rocked my world and my writing. I graduated as Mr. Hersey retired; we wrote letters back and forth until he died, and when I sent him stories, he never failed to see through the armature of particulars to the heart of the work itself.

Arguments about any kind of exceptionality are dangerous, which is why I am not generalizing here. But as much as "race work" is my work, it also is important to debunk the illusion that there are not crossings that happen all the time. White people and white men as a class are at the root of many of our problems, but there are also white men who are not saddled with racial issues and obsessions, or at least know how to suppress or transcend them when engaged in the necessary work of mentoring. I haven't counted the black friends of any of these men and do not know if I am the only young black woman they have ever mentored, what they think about Israelis and Palestinians, jazz and hip-hop, Wright vs. Ellison, Malcolm vs. Martin, if they give to the NAACP.

You see, I don't think doing the right thing has to be all that difficult. I don't think most young people are hard to love and respect at all. One of the great shames of racism, especially as it entwines with class prejudice, is how it teaches people to see young people of color—to see children—as dangerous, unlovable beasts. Our communities need to constantly reaffirm the sacred covenants of mentorship, of elders caring for younger people who are not their biological children. I want to imagine for a moment that if I have known these particular men, then the world is full of them, people who are men and who are white who took one young black woman seriously, and taught her, and loved her. Uncle Herbie, Bill, Professor B., Mr. Hersey: These are the white men who in some ways, in their ways, helped me become a black feminist, because they helped me to become.

# CARTILAGE

## Susan Straight

"Girl, we can't have the Disco Ball on Saturday before Labor Day," I said. "Won't we all be cooking for The Hole?" When everyone looked at me, I added, "We're the old folks now. Right?"

We are in our early and late forties, and our children and grandchildren milled about outside the community room at the park where we'd gathered to make our plans. Most of us have lived here, in Riverside, California, for all our lives, have known one another since we were children or teens or just-married, and all the women around the table started laughing when I showed my palms to the sky in question of our status. My friend Revia said, "Since last year we are."

Last Labor Day, we realized that all the aunts and uncles and elders who used to have holiday celebrations in someone's driveway or yard had passed on or moved away to quieter places. So we took over, barbecuing and cooking side dishes and bringing tables and chairs to this park, to a sunken spot we call The Hole because it's down the slope of an arroyo and shaded by huge pecan trees.

In the seventies, many white people in this city used to be afraid to drive past this park because black teenagers sometimes threw rocks at pale faces in luxury cars. But now, the neighborhood known as the Eastside, where my husband and many of my friends grew up, is shifting from African-American to Mexican-born, and the whole city is as integrated as our old neighborhoods always were.

Today, the familiar faces I have known nearly all my life, descended from men and women born in Louisiana, Oklahoma, Mississippi, and Georgia, are all around me at this table as we plan fund-raisers for a group formed to keep the old neighborhood alive through dinners and talent shows and community projects.

And me, always the only white person in the room, with blond hair, blue eyes, and black-rimmed glasses instead of the granny specs some of the women in this room teased me for when we were in junior high.

Back then, when I met my future husband, his skin red-brown as palm bark, his natural wide enough to frame my face when we stood in front of a mirror, a few of these women gave me a hard time, and I knew to expect it. I knew what they thought of white girls.

In junior high and then high school, I'd watched closely the chameleonlike shifts in clothes, voice, hair, and attitude as people decided how they would transform themselves into who they thought they wanted to be. A few white girls considered themselves Chicanas, and matched their friends' wire-thin eyebrows, dark lipstick, and babydoll tanks covered with flannel Pendletons. A few black girls were cheerleaders and looked exactly like their white counterparts, with tight ponytails and great posture and matching overalls. A few Chicano guys were black gangsters, and one black guy from my old neighborhood was a vato. Stoners and cholos and letterman jocks—all had uniforms, theme songs, and secret code words sprinkled in their conversations. They all had their territories on campus, too—the hill, the arcade, the brick wall, and the parking lot.

The white girls who wanted to be black, before the nineties when the word "wigger" came into play, worked very hard, but as I watched, I had the feeling they were going about it all wrong.

They talked as if born in Mississippi. They cornrowed their brown or red hair, and their scalps shone white as mother-of-pearl in the gaps. They snapped their fingers and sat at the right table, but they were never quite comfortable there, because most of the black girls didn't trust them at all.

For good reason. When one of the white girls, upper-middle class, not from my mixed neighborhood or from the Eastside, decided she really wanted to be homecoming queen her senior year, she went right out and got a blond escort from the crosstown rival and wealthier high school. Her hair blow-dried straight, her lipstick pink, she was transformed back into her true self. And she got her butt kicked. Her transformation and betrayal were so obvious and egregious she became legend: to do what she did was called "pulling a Sheila."

Even then, knowing I'd probably marry my boyfriend, I watched. I was so pale, so blond, and I wished I at least had black hair, darker eyebrows. But having had girlfriends since junior high who'd taught me how to dance in the gym and during PE, who sat patiently with me during class and braided hair and told stories, I thought my caution and observance might help when I knew nothing of my physical appearance would.

He was sixteen, I was fifteen, and on Labor Day in 1976, he

brought me to his parents' house, where—no pressure—everyone gathered in the driveway and the living room. About a hundred people, all staring at the little blond girl with a halter dress and nervous smile. One of those white girls, I knew they were thinking.

The aunts, eight of them, stared me down in the living room, but nodded and shook my hand. But his sister and cousins and stepsister and other girls were in the dining room, girls my age who didn't trust me for a minute. They cut their eyes my way, muttered things not quite under their breaths, and elbowed me out of the way after refusing my hand. They sucked their teeth instead, along with a few female neighbors who raised their eyebrows and said, "Mmm, mmm, mmm. What does he think he's doing?"

And what did I think I was doing? How could they not think I was pulling a Sheila? I headed for the kitchen out of instinct. I knew what to do.

My mother is Swiss. I am the oldest of all her children, birth and foster, and I have been cooking and cleaning since I was seven. When my future husband introduced me to his mother, holding court at the stove where she fed not only her own six kids but half the neighborhood, she looked into my face and said graciously, "Let's get you a plate."

I said, "Can I help you with the dishes?"

She stood near me at the Formica counters and stove the same color as my mother's. I exclaimed over the barbecue and helped her cut the ham and asked how she made monkey bread, her famous circle of rolls. At Thanksgiving, then Christmas, and on Super Bowl Sunday (a family holiday with the same importance as the others), I washed dishes and stayed in the kitchen with the women, who followed my future mother-in-law's noddings and finally accepted me, after a period of intense observation.

And my own mother, who stands four-eleven, looked up at the tall brown boy who came to pick me up and said, "You're on the basketball team?" Anyone who played a sport, and was of reasonable height, was fine with her. He didn't drink, smoke, or do anything to hurt his basketball career, and our first dates consisted of shooting hoops at the playground and then playing tennis at the university courts.

She accepted him without reservation. During our senior year, she came to his basketball games, knitting in the stands a few rows below his father, who sat with cronies in trench coats to conceal their flasks, shouting, "Fall, ball!" whenever his son lofted a shot.

During all those years, I did listen to the same music, and we danced the same dances, and used the same secret code words of the neighborhood. How could we have talked otherwise? But I never cornrowed my hair or pretended that I was not half Swiss. I was always too skinny. I still am.

I have been an honorary Eastsider for twenty-five years now. We all wear jeans or comfortable pants to our many gatherings, and even though I have been divorced for five years, my daughters and I are expected at each and every event. Most of the time, we all wear our hair in buns, because we are at that stage in our lives. We are kind of tired, and we've been cooking all day.

We sit around the table today: Doris and Revia, whose mother was born in Louisiana but has lived at the end of this block for forty-five years. Revia's daughters and nieces, who all call me Auntie. My sister-in-law Tina, and my brother-in-law's girlfriend Shirley, whose father was born in the South and whose mother was born in Mexico. Her tamales and temper are legendary, and though they never married, my children call her Auntie.

The Aunties. That's what we are now, and we have earned the status. We bring one another food when someone is sick or someone has died. We sit companionably and holler at the kids to keep it down.

We direct the younger girls not to walk too far from where we are in the park. And I laugh inside when I watch the rare white teen, girl or boy, try to navigate the hundred-plus people of Labor Day or August Family Reunion. They have the right jackets, carry the proper CDs, and have cornrows or tattoos.

But they don't have stretch marks, knife cuts from dissembling hams and chicken, laugh lines and frown marks from our children and spouses, sore backs from carrying wet laundry, and sore feet from carrying babies and pacing sidelines and grocery lines.

"How did we get to be the old folks?" Shirley asked, laughing and yet a deep furrow between her brows. We were watching teenagers gather around the table in The Hole, irritating us with their loudness and greedy helpings, just the way we used to get on the aunts' nerves.

I shrugged, and Revia did, too.

" 'Cause nobody else stepped in."

On Labor Day, our knees met in a companionable semicircle, a crescent grin of white plastic chairs arranged on the slope of the depression under the pecan trees, where we can keep an eye on the food. We are in charge. We brought macaroni and cheese, pineapple upside-down cake, potato salads, and string beans with ham hocks. I brought rice and blackeyed peas and hot sausage, my dish, the one people ask if I am bringing. Along with the scars, you'd better have a dish.

I am still blond and small, and my women friends and sister-in-law and relatives are not, but our arms rest alongside one another's on the chairs' plastic smoothness, and they are all alike. Sun-marked, softer than when we were young, our knuckles bigger, our fingers sore. We talk about our hurts. My feet, Shirley's wrists, Doris's back, and Revia's migraines.

A white family shows up, friends of someone's, and their teenage boy stares at me when introductions are made. He has on the right football jersey, the right haircut, the right tattoos. I nod at him, and we watch him get a plate of food with our nephews. He says, "This looks really good. Thank you."

From our vantage point, we raise our brows and smile.

My house is a mile-and-a-half from the park, not on the Eastside. Half of us don't live in the neighborhood anymore, but we gather there and our hearts remain there.

My three daughters have lived in the same house for four-teen years, and they have friends from our neigborhood. Half Mexican, half white. Half Salvadoran, half Polish. Half Saudi, half black.

My girls are Swiss, French, African, Creek, Cherokee, and Irish. They don't judge their friends, or themselves, by music or clothes or hairstyles. They listen to Nickelback and Lenny Kravitz and Santana and the Dixie Chicks. They roll their eyes at their father and me when we play the Bar-Kays and Parliament. They roll their eyes at white teens who cruise by our house in expensive trucks, blaring Jay-Z and Snoop Dogg and shouting, "What up, dog?"

They suck their teeth and say, "Not you," and in their tone, I hear the voices of their actual ancestors and their mother's friends, the women who sit in the circle with me. We know it's all about the scars and pain, the food and laughs, the secret code you can only understand when you've bumped elbows while standing at the stove, when you've sat by the hospital bed while someone you loved was fading away—places where it doesn't matter what you wear or listen to or how your hair looks. It matters that your knees touch while you wait.

# BATTLEFIELDS, OR IS FRIENDSHIP GREATER THAN THE COLONIAL AND DOMINATING RACE IDEOLOGIES OF HUNDREDS OF YEARS?

## Luis Rodriguez

When my friend Tony underwent a particularly contentious divorce—including a custody battle for his daughter and stepdaughter—I tried to be someone he could turn to for support and, oddly enough, to share tears. Men aren't supposed to do that. But Tony and I have always had a close emotional bond—through thirty years of struggles with our wives, work, politics, kids.

We weren't always good fathers, husbands, or even friends—but we learned.

Tony is a fellow ex-steelworker turned writer and political revolutionary. Of Jewish-Italian descent—a "white" guy—he became godfather to my oldest son, Ramiro, and I became godfather to his daughter Michaela. Compadres and comrades. However, if my environment had won, he should never have occupied this role in my life. The fact is, for most of my young life, I hated and mistrusted white people—and for good reason.

As a brown-skinned Mexican migrant to Los Angeles in the mid-fifties, I had to negotiate the treacherous racial and economic class realities of the United States at the time. It was 1956—and I was two—when my family moved from Ciudad Juarez, Chihuahua, Mexico, to Los Angeles. By 1956, Martin Luther King Jr. had barely begun the Birmingham marches. Rosa Parks had only recently fought to sit in the front of the bus. Cesar Chavez was still a Pachuco-dressed teen in the farm fields of California.

The first day of school, the teacher sent me to the back of the class because I didn't speak English. For most of that year, I ended up in a corner, building blocks. If I uttered a Spanish word, I would get scolded or swatted. Although my first year of schooling was in a predominantly African-American elementary school in South Central LA, in my second year my family moved to a middle-class all-white community in the San Fernando Valley where my father had a position teaching Spanish to high school students.

I recall getting chased and beaten for being Mexican. Once, I raised my hand to be excused to use the bathroom. The teacher refused to let me go, and I peed in my pants. Then she roughly pushed me to the corner as the other kids yelled "PU!" Later, at age nine, after my dad lost the teaching job and declared bankruptcy, we ended up in the mostly poor Mexican community of South San Gabriel in the East Los Angeles area.

The whites we knew there were the teachers who told us what to do, the police who beat us, or the welfare or social worker who periodically checked in on us.

Once we met a "nice" white person, one of my sister's teachers, who acted like she really liked us but had my mother sew and iron her clothes while my brother and I were taken to her house to clean the yard.

In our reality, whites held the power over our lives (even if it wasn't all whites, since there were whites who lived in the same miserable conditions we did). The rest of us could reign within certain allowable parameters, but these "whites" held the power over the best housing, the best schools, the best jobs.

My few white friends were poor, remnants of the old "Okie" or Jewish families still in the barrio. But most didn't stay long.

Caucasian people in Los Angeles tended to amalgamate into becoming "white" or "Anglo," even if they had no English background (many were Irish, German, Italian, or other European descent). Mexicans, however, were Mexican. Japanese were Japanese. Blacks were Black. These lines fell into neat categories of color: white, brown, yellow, and black (although over the years the lines became more complicated with the arrival of Southeast Asian, Central American, Korean, Russian, and Armenian immigrants into LA).

I didn't create this world—I fell into it as soon as I arrived in the United States.

I learned to hate white people. I say "learned" because I didn't start out that way. The few whites who stayed in the barrio and got initiated into the gang were exceptions—they were "homies." But if we dared to step out of our dirt-road, lean-to neighborhoods to the well-paved, stuccoed homes of the "Gabachos" (as some Mexicans would call whites), we were in for trouble—police harassment or encounters with white gangs.

Of course, they were in danger from us, too.

In the barrio gang, we burglarized the fancy homes in the white communities; we mugged whites at newly constructed malls or took them on at high school football games. In the early days the battles were between "Surfers" and "Beaners." Surfers were the "good guys." You can guess who the Beaners were.

Of course, not every Mexican hated whites or vice versa. Many learned to live with one another, adopt each other's ways and languages, even intermarry. Unfortunately, what assimilation did exist for Mexicans included degrading things like refusing to speak Spanish, claiming to be of Spanish or Italian descent, or becoming more anti-Mexican than racist whites.

I hated those Mexicans as much as I hated whites.

The degradation of Mexican culture was thorough. We weren't recognized in school, in history or social studies, on television or in the movies (except as lowly laborers or banditos). In history classes, the only two times Mexicans were mentioned included bloodthirsty Aztecs who took out people's hearts. However, these accounts came from Spanish sources and have been challenged by anthropologists who see this as an excuse for the more destructive "human sacrifice" the Spanish were doing to the indigenous populations. The other mention was the Battle of the Alamo, where "heroic" Anglo Americans like Davy Crockett and Jim Bowie unsuccessfully fought off a larger force of Mexicans. Of course, most of the history books failed to point out that Crockett, Bowie, and the American force (which also consisted of Mexicans against the rule of Mexican dictator Santa Ana) had come to rip off Texas from Mexico so it would become a slave territory for the slave-owning power of the American South (which is precisely what happened).

Today, two major historical monuments—the Little Big Horn ("Custer's Last Stand") and the Alamo—exist not to honor the victors, but to honor the Anglo-Saxon vanquished.

In my youth, these were issues of dignity, of fairness, of something basic and intrinsic to human nature. I knew then that racism and the resultant humiliations were wrong, and in time whites became my enemies.

In jail, whites were the targets. In the barrio gang, I struck fear in their hearts. Only cops could really take us on (and we gave them a hard time—ambushing them, shooting at their police units, and targeting the overhead police helicopters that inspected the barrio every night). White racism became a major reason that I hated the social and economic world I had inherited—and that I had sworn to tear down.

This was, as Malcolm X stated, "the hate that hate produced."

But while hate can awaken you, keep you alive, and prevent you from succumbing to a crushingly numb silence, it can also fuck you up.

Years later, I recall a group of African Americans and Chicanos hitting hard on some white people during a conference. But their rage was largely cerebral. I got up and said, "You hate white people so much—you don't know what hate is. If I could get a gun and kill every white person, I would. If I could

find a way to obliterate their conquests, their colonial domination, the imposed authority and lies—I would. There just ain't
enough bullets in the world to deal with my rage."

It's a rage that I had to turn into something else or be poi-
soned by it for the rest of my life, which didn't mean I was
turning to superficial love and tolerance—until my dying
breath I will never tolerate racism, poverty, injustice, and the
Euro-centered capitalist, material-based value system we live
under. It meant looking at the roots and foundations of racism
and learning how to eradicate that vs. just hating people.

For me, the turning point came in the late 1960s and early
1970s. The civil rights, treaty rights, anticolonial, and land
grant battles of African Americans, women, Chicanos, Puerto
Ricans, and Native Americans were in full swing. Everyone
seemed to be fighting inside his or her own turf. But some
issues pulled us together, like the Vietnam War, poverty, and
equality. I first got politicized during that period—it was then
that I learned to turn the hatred I had toward whites to a more
strategic and politically astute understanding of the class
nature of our struggles.

I met Tony during that period. Originally from the
Venice–Culver City section of Los Angeles, Tony ended up in
an East Los Angeles housing project where we organized radical youth activities that spread throughout the Los Angeles
area. Tony attended a meeting of community leaders in East
LA, one of the few white people in attendance. He was forth-
right and intelligent, not condescending or awestruck as many
white radicals tended to be. In time, our mutual love of struggle and revolution, and our intense engagements in such struggle, brought us together.

We labored in a paper mill and a steel mill together, among the least well-paid members of the working class as well as the unemployed whom we also helped organize. We'd sit around and analyze the world from the prism of assembly line reality. While politics bonded us, it was humor that kept us going until the end of a long graveyard shift—or on our days off, late nights drinking and talking.

In this work, except in some skilled crafts, whites worked alongside people of color. The economy didn't care about racism—in many industries, the need for an integrated workforce pitted capitalists and corporate heads against segregation. This was the last important time, from a historical point of view, that a section of capitalists had a commonality of struggle in this country with a section of workers.

Our other friends included a Hopi-Laguna Indian from an East LA housing project and an African American from South Central. Together we stormed the gates of city hall, the Los Angeles school board, corporate offices, and the offices of racist landlords. We took on the system and survived to mature, get smarter, master words and thought, and keep on struggling.

By the 1980s, however, industry was undergoing the most dramatic changes in more than one hundred years. Advanced tools and cheaper markets forced many plants to close down across the land, in particular the Midwest, but also throughout Los Angeles, which saw the closing of auto plants, tire factories, foundries, the large steel manufacturing plants like Bethlehem and American Bridge, and aerospace production sites.

Around this time, in 1980, I quit industrial work and started to focus on my writing. Tony also pursued writing even while he continued his factory work. By the mid-eighties, I landed in Chicago where Tony had moved for work, to organize and to start a family. We wrote for local and national newspapers.

I dealt with African Americans, whites, Asians, Mexicans, Puerto Ricans, and others in labor struggles, against homelessness, for immigrant rights, against prisons, and for youth. Of my three wives, my second, Paulette, was African American (although my family's earlier relationships with blacks were also strained due to the intense competition at the bottom of the social ladder). And my work among youth gangs in Los Angeles and Chicago was done in all communities.

For me, the color of one's skin stopped being paramount. The initiative, creativity, and intelligence that one brought to these struggles were more important. Whites stopped being enemies just because they were white—and a world opened up with more infinite possibilities for change and progress than most people could imagine in the sixties and seventies.

Besides, by hating all whites, one creates a more formidable monolith than what really exists. "Whites" have differing interests, politics, and beliefs; some of them can help tear down the whole system of white dominance and present-day economic exploitation. It's ironic how some white supremacists and people who hate whites end up in the same place in this regard—creating in their minds a compact "white" community.

Another consideration is how much hating white people can become an all-consuming passion. It takes too much energy. This hate can take you off track from knowing yourself and your own realities. It places "whites" in a special place in one's heart and mind—a place that should only be occupied by what you really love. As the Native American poet and activist John Trudell said, this kind of hate becomes devotional.

Of course, there are people who love to hate.


Do I hate whites now? I don't like them or dislike them. I know the history that created the "white" category in this world and that also created the brown, yellow, and black ones. None of these have any true biological, anthropological, or spiritual basis.

I judge so-called white people as I do everyone else—by their actions, their visions, their truths, their relationships. I have three granddaughters who have Irish, Hungarian, and German ancestry along with their indigenous Mexican (my one grandson is Puerto Rican and Mexican). I love them just the same. I work with whites and others in helping youth, and in the mentoring and cultural work I do. Many young people have been given a leg up because of these efforts.

I don't hate whites. I don't love them.

I do oppose racism and poverty. I will always challenge the machinations and consequences of a profit-driven social and economic system we are presently bound to. I also understand that most poor people in the United States are whites—we have more in common in this sense than we have differences due to skin pigmentation. Divisions—between those of color and those who are white—continue to impede our progress as a people.

Mostly, however, I love family. I love our dreams. I love our gifts and passions. I love the connectiveness we all have to all beings and things and the daily miracles that come with life. I love the fight to bring true equity and justice in this world. I love writing and art and aligning with the creative powers in the universe and in the most minute substances of existence.

And I value friendship like that with Tony.

Tony and I have had many good times together. He's a funny dude, a born mimic. He even mimics me (although, in my opinion, he does a bad job). We've driven across various sections of this country—from Los Angeles to Chicago, Los Angeles to San Francisco, New York City to Chicago. We would evaluate everything on those trips—movies, bands, songs, books, women—I swear we solved most of the world's problems several times over. Nothing like a long trip across this country's immense terrain to clear up ideas, habits, memories, and plans.

And we've had our disagreements, including times when I think Tony's "whiteness" had informed a statement or decision he made. Tony can be arrogant and superior-minded at times, forcing me to "bring him down" to the real world, so to speak. But, again, these are superficial concerns—our deep ties have overcome many of them.

Tony is now a lawyer in Northern California, having finished law school at age forty-five. I remember being overjoyed at his graduation; I knew how hard it was for this working-class man to get to this point. He is one "white" guy who turned to the dispossessed and disenfranchised—to fight with the oppressed and exploited—and remove the veil of whiteness that others have failed to do. I have had other white friendships and partnerships, but Tony has been the closest and most consistent.

Friendship is greater than the colonial and dominating race ideologies of hundreds of years. We can forget this sometimes when we get trapped in the battlefields of race and gender politics—a battlefield our social and political enemies have set up and can win on. In the thoughts, feelings, and being we all share as humans, we can germinate the seeds that can remove the color features of our divisions so we can find real differentiation in what truly matters—to live whole and complete lives and for others to do the same.

It's what Tony would want for me—and what I would ever want for Tony. Not a "white" guy, my friend.

# REPELLENT AFRO

## Trey Ellis

I began, typically enough for a black child of the sixties, at Howard University Hospital. My parents had been Howard undergrads, and my father was in the medical school there when I was born. In the first five years of my life, we moved from D.C., to Dayton, to Detroit. The three cities have more in common than alliteration. They are typically urban, that is, as black as they can be—"chocolate cities." Leaving Detroit was the end of my typical African-American childhood. It would not be for another twenty years, while I was hitchhiking across Africa, that my skin color would resemble that of the majority of the people around me.

We moved from Detroit to Ypsilanti, Michigan, a depressed, working-class suburb of Ann Arbor. My father was accepted into a psychiatric residency at the University of Michigan, and my mother decided to complete her master's in psychology there. It was 1967, they were in their late twenties, black and middle class, but this was the first time in their lives that they had ever left the comfort of predominantly black surroundings. My little sister was four and I was going on six. My parents had discovered what was at the time this revolutionary new concept in living: a subdivision of "town homes," tiny, semi-prefabricated, faux Tudor house-lets mashed together by the half dozen and replicated dozens and dozens of times for acre upon acre on what used to be rich Midwestern famland. Across Geddes Road were the real houses, small and dingy, while our new homes of the future, though slapped together and most still under construction, represented eastern Michigan's bright and shining future (by way of Elizabethan England). We were one of the first to move in, for years the only African Americans in a utopia of eager, young, multiracial families.

The problem was that most of the people in town were poor and undereducated and worked for GM's Willow Springs plant. I was lonely at first in the near-vacant subdivision, my old (black) friends from Detroit coming to visit me or me them only once or twice a year. Gradually, the place started to fill up with auto worker families hankering for a bit of fine, faux Tudor living. One of those families was the Jacksons, recently from Birmingham, Alabama. Despite their last name, they were as white as rice, including Lynn Jackson, who must have been in the sixth grade, had long brown hair down to her butt, and whom I loved desperately. Her younger brother, Scott, was a year ahead of me, but we became best friends mainly because we didn't have many other kids to choose from. Scott loved the South, and his favorite game to play with me was one of his own invention. He would mount his Stingray and chase me in and around the rows of as-yet-uncompleted townhouses shouting, "I'm Robert E. Lee and I'm gonna git ya!" Though he was much bigger than I was, I, rode my Huffy "Cheetah Slic" faster and managed to get away from him, usually. I loved to taunt him with shouts of "I'm Ulysses S. Grant and we won the war!"

This would make him turn red and maybe even crash his bike. I don't think he ever called me "nigger," though he would slip sometimes and say it about somebody else. I think I remember him apologizing afterward, usually, but what I remember much more deeply is how the word echoed inside me, liquefying some inner part of me that was supposed to be solid.

I was just about to write that though my parents often invited Scott over to play in our twenty-foot-square, fenced-in yard, his father never invited me to play in their identical one. Yet I don't quite remember if that is true. Scott's father did have a Galaxy 500 convertible. Green, I believe. Perhaps it was *my* parents who were skittish of Mr. Jackson, him coming from Alabama and all. Memory is as reliable as the wind, and memory about race is even more prone to gusts of paranoia and exaggeration.

Well, when Scott and I weren't fighting, we were best friends and would rope the more impressionable kids in the subdivision into dirt clod or crabapple fights or run into the vast woods just across the way and pick berries or climb impossibly tall trees. Summertime in Michigan and night wouldn't fall till after ten, so we could play after dinner in the twilight till mother after mother stood on her porch and cried out the name of her child.

One day, Scott and I had wandered far from Geddes Road, by a river somewhere, next to an abandoned factory. We came upon a dozen or so black kids. I didn't know we had that many of us on the side of town that Scott and I lived on. We didn't. That was how far we had wandered. The black kids, much bigger than me and even bigger and generally older than Scott, quickly encircled him and punched him bloody. They didn't seem to see me at all. Because my presence challenged the rules of their universe, they simply ignored me. And I was too scared to make myself known. Perhaps that is where it began. Now, after years of being the "one in the group who was not like the other," I have perfected the art of camouflage. To this day, although I am a six-foot-two-inch black man, I can still disappear at will.

Or perhaps I just stood there because a part of me wanted to pound Scott Jackson myself.

Soon the beating was over and they left, swaggering and grumbling more insults. I rushed to my friend and helped him up and onto his bike.

A little while later, my father got a job at Yale and we moved to Hamden, Connecticut, the dinky suburb next to New Haven, the college town. Our part of Hamden was 100 percent white. My parents chose it because it had the best elementary school in the area. They didn't seem to consider the problems my sister and I might have trying to find friends in a working-class Italian- and Irish-American neighborhood.

Since leaving Detroit, I had metamorphosed from a regular old black kid into what I would refer to, in a 1988 article entitled "The New Black Aesthetic," as a "cultural mulatto." I was equally uncomfortable in the world of pizza parlors and duckpin bowling alleys of southern Connecticut as I was visiting my grandparents in either Dayton or West Philadelphia. Back in Hamden at my new elementary school, it was not unusual for me to be called "Oreo" by some black kid who was bused to school, and "nigger" by some "Italian Stallion" wannabe in the same week. Deracinated and adrift, I was a wreck. After reading *Hamlet*, I knew that I had found my literary soul mate, and alone at night in my room, I luxuriated in the self-pity of calling myself "The Melancholy Black Dane."

After a false start with the racist Irish kid next door, and remembering how unsatisfying and confusing a friendship like that had been with Scott, I decided to seek out a whole different type of white kid: Jews. They lived across Whitney Avenue (named after the inventor of the cotton gin), in much nicer homes than on our side, but still, I had so much more in common with them than with the garden-variety white kids who surrounded us. We were all upwardly mobile, children of McGovern supporters, and obnoxiously arrogant about our intellect. And of course we were all different from the majority. The country club near where the Jewish kids lived, "High Lane," didn't have any Jewish members until the Tofflers joined in the mid-seventies. The rest of the Jews and the Ellises all swam and played tennis farther down the road, at Ridge Top.

Mike Zeagan's father was a psychiatrist who worked with my dad, and we were both precocious smart-asses. In the fifth grade, we adapted and staged the made-for-TV movie *Brian's Song*, recording it on a wonderful new medium, videotape. I starred as Chicago Bears running back Gayle Sayers, and Alan Lowenstein was running back Brian Piccolo. They were the first NFL black and white players to room with each before Piccolo died of cancer.

The competing gang of smart kids, the "Queer Club," we called them, lived not too far from Mike, and we would often cross paths and antagonize each other. David Kennedy, Ben Sandweiss, Danny Workman, and the other six or seven in the Queer Club would surround Mike and me, and we would have an epic rumble of the nerds. One of them, I forget who, threw a stick at my then considerable Afro. The stick bounced off, and the other kids doubled over laughing. "Repellent Afro" they called me as they hurled more shit at my head. Shame washed over me like hot soup. Shame sucked all the fight out of me. I just wanted to disappear again and wait for them to leave.

Though I was a year older than Mike, he was the boss of our two-man outfit, and David Kennedy was the boss of the Queer Club. I was bigger than Mike, and Ben Sandweiss was bigger than David, so both of us were sort of the muscle of our little sixth grade mini-gangs. During one recess, after months of battling each other, we all decided that Ben and I should wrestle to see whose side was the winner. Remembering how they laughed at my "repellent Afro," I pinned him easily, and he howled like a rat caught in a trap. Then a few weeks later in the advanced social studies class, he was the captain of one trivia team and I was the captain of the other. We were soon in a deadlock, going back and forth, back and forth, each getting an answer correct. The rest of the kids were soon bored. Ben and I, however, were battling to the death. Then the teacher asked him who lived at 10 Downing Street, and he didn't know. I jumped in, won the game, and crushed him again.

Of our entire public school, we were the only two who were going to Hopkins, a private school in New Haven, the next year. Our parents, who had no idea about our rivalry, thought we should get together. First his parents took me to a play, then a few weeks later, Ben came and spent the night. We couldn't sleep, couldn't stop talking about every book we had ever read and how stupid everybody else in the world was. Around dawn, both of us hoarse from talking, we walked around the block, talking still, in our bathrobes and slippers, then made Leggo waffles and waited for my family to get up. Finally, I'd found somebody who seemed to understand how fucking hard it was being eleven.

That summer, Mike and I ran into the Queer Club, and one of them threatened to throw something at my Afro again, but this time, Ben told the kid to quit being such a jerk. That was about thirty years ago, and we've been best friends ever since. Danny Workman also defected from the Queer Club, and the three of us did everything together throughout high school and are still as close as brothers. We all even married within months of one another. Ben, who is half Jewish, half WASP, was the leader, the one who came up with all the deviant ideas like breaking into Yale's Harkness tower in the middle of the night, or prying open some Yalie snack bar that had been pad-locked for the summer. I was in the middle and liked to think of myself as the voice of reason, but in general I was more just the worrywart. Danny was a year younger than us and lived with his mom and his three brothers and sisters after the divorce. It was 1973, and Ben, Danny, and I would have a blast staying up late at Danny's father's hippie parties full of earnest grad students and unwashed mandolin players.

Back at my house, my parents' interaction with each other had only two levels of volume: shrieking and glacial silence. The tension was crushing me, so I avoided it whenever I could, sleeping over at Ben or Danny's many nights of the week. Ben's house wasn't much quieter because Ben, each and every week-end, would insist on sleeping in until his mother flung open the door and screeched at him to get his butt out of bed, and that went also for his "no-good, lazy friends." Danny's house was ruled by his vastly outnumbered and overwhelmed single mother, so it was much easier to be a kid there.

I think it was around 1974 that I was convinced that race as a concept would soon extinguish itself. I was sure that my generation had finally licked the problem that had so vexed everyone from Lincoln to Du Bois to my dad. My father, however, was much more old school, and was always telling me to watch out for slights. He reminded me, as his parents had reminded him, that the color of my skin was a burden that I would overcome only through dedication to study so rigorous that it would ultimately compel white people to realize how wonderfully capable I was. "White folks," he often began a sentence, and usually ended it by reminding me that while "they" might not expect much from a little black child, he would expect nothing less than my best. I thought he was an old square, hopelessly behind the times. I was fourteen. He was thirty-six.

When I was a teenager, my parents decided to try to force some black friends on me. Jack & Jill is a black bourgeois organization created for kids exactly like me, but I rebelled mightily. Every time my parents would drive me way across town to play on some other bougie black kid's trampoline, I made it a point never to give the kid a chance. I felt like they were trying to arrange a marriage and were willing to trade me for a bucket of beads and a cow. Besides, I already had my best friends and didn't need anybody else. After all, my own home was so tense and gloomy that Ben and Danny's families became my own. I felt absolutely, one hundred percent accepted by them and still do, and make a point of visiting both their parents whenever I'm back in town.

Danny had a small sailboat, and we would take the bus out to the very Italian neighborhood of East Haven, then have to walk about a half mile to the New Haven yacht club. It was always scary because East Haven had a very bad rep, but one day it got much, much worse. Six thick-necked creeps, looking like they walked right out of *Saturday Night Fever*, saw me and started shouting, "Hey! Go back to the Congo!" They looked like grown-ups, or at least seniors. For a moment, I thought all they wanted to do was yell. Then they started running. We ran, too, never as fast in our lives, down alleys, over fences, all the way to the boat landing. Though we never talked about it, I remember how grateful I was that they were there with me. It wasn't lost on me that Danny and Ben didn't just watch, as I had done when the black kids had pounded on that defender of Robert E. Lee—my old best friend back in Michigan, Scott Jackson.

Still, I never shared my blackness with them. We never discussed race except dismissively: "I don't think of you as black. You're just Trey." Or, "I'm not even *really* Jewish. I'm just a person." For us, somehow, talking about our differences felt tacky. We deftly avoided the subject, the way cultured grown-ups avoid talking about how much money they make. I didn't tell them that I felt so nervous that I was almost sick whenever a Toys "R" Us assistant manager followed me around the store, and that I wouldn't breathe right again until I was back out on the street. I didn't tell them that I had been reading *Soul on Ice*, or *The Autobiography of Malcolm X*, or listening to Richard Pryor albums every day after school. My blackness was my secret world, hidden and deliciously, transgressively pleasurable. My blackness was my pornography.

The secret didn't come out until we finally started to date. There was only one other black girl besides my sister in my private school, Stephanie Brown. I didn't really know her at all, but I figured she was pretty cute, and all the other boys in school were starting to ask girls out, so I figured I kind of had to. So after some coaching from my mother and vicious teasing from my little sister, I called her and kinda-sorta asked her out. Actually, I just mumbled something and hung up quickly when I interpreted her too-long pause as a rejection.

Afterward, my mother and father both told me that they wouldn't be surprised if I dated white girls. Though they weren't overly pleased with the idea, they realized that, statistically, they had almost guaranteed that outcome when they chose to move us to Hamden. To surprise them, to spite them, I never even tried. I told myself that the reason for my celibacy was that I was a closet nationalist in a sea of white girls, but the real reason was that I was terrified. My "principled" stance was just an excuse for my cowardice.

There was one white girl, however, that Danny, Ben, and I all secretly loved. Melissa Paulsen was naturally gorgeous and funny, too smart and a little bit sad, just like us. Then that summer Danny, Ben, and Melissa all took sailing lessons. I don't remember what I was doing instead, but I can tell you that, twenty-five-years later, I still regret not joining them. Every night, I would hear about Melissa in her cutoff shorts and how Ben and Danny were each getting up the courage to ask her out. On the day that Ben said he was finally going to do it, Danny beat him to it. For a week or two, Danny, who had always been the junior member of our group because he was a year younger, was the king of the world. Ben was miserable (and of course so was I, but I never told them that I loved her, too). Then one night, Danny called me in tears. Melissa was acting strangely. He was sure that she'd found somebody else. Then there was a beep on my phone line (we had just gotten this new service called call waiting). I switched over to the other line and heard Ben gloat, "I just made out with her, it was fantastic." I didn't feel sorry for Danny. I felt sorry for myself, that I was on the outside of this love triangle and didn't see any way of ever getting in. She seemed like the perfect girl for me, and I still wonder whatever became of her.

My loneliness, romantic and otherwise, and the bleakness of the local dating scene were my main reasons for transferring from Hopkins to Phillips Academy, Andover. My parents thought it was my competitive desire to see, after I had academically outperformed most of the upper-middle-class kids at Hopkins, if I could hold my own with the John Kennedy Jrs. and the so-and-so Rockefellers. My parents did not understand me at all. The most important reason I had for changing schools was that, statistically, I'd have a better shot at finally getting laid.

Ben's big brother had transferred to Andover years before, and Ben decided to make the move, too. Though I was about the only nonscholarship black student there, I was, for the first time since leaving Detroit eleven years earlier, not the only black kid in most of my classes. We had our Afro-Latino-American center, Af-Lat-Am, a creaky, Revolutionary-era home famous for its great dances. Ben and I were still best friends, but suddenly I had a black community that I could be a part of as well. Though I didn't make any lasting black friendships there, my statistical gamble about black girls finally, sort of, paid off. Joy Anderson sewed her own Naugahyde pants (in the dark they looked just like leather, I swear), and she wore them to all Af-Lat-Am dances. Watching her move in them changed the rhythm of my heart, and after two years, I finally got up the courage to ask her out. On the very last day of school, she gave me my first kiss. Even though Ben and Danny had both already lost their virginity years before, and my entire relationship with Joy consisted of a few slow dances and this one kiss, I still felt that I was finally on the road to catching up.

When I got to Stanford, the black community was even larger than Andover's. We even had our own dorm, and I decided to stay there, to live with my own for a change. Unfortunately, most of the black students in the dorm, called Ujamaa, a Swahili word for cooperative economics, took one look at my Top-Siders and either dismissed me or ridiculed me mercilessly as a preppy Tom sellout. It is a cliché but still true that the most radical black kids on campus are often the ones who grew up just like me but who affect a "superblackness" to protect themselves from total assimilation. They made my freshman year hell, rolling their eyes and pointing at me whenever they talked about "some brothers having a problem looking at themselves in the mirror."

To save myself, I took refuge in the Stanford *Chaparral*, the campus humor magazine. My good friends, for the most part, were white kids on the magazine, and they're still some of my very best friends. By this point, I was much more comfortable bringing the totality of my being to these relationships, so in some ways they're more honest than my friendships with Danny and Ben. As usual, I was the only black kid on the staff, but I didn't care. Eventually, I became the second black editor in the magazine's history. For my first editorial, I turned the "old boy," the court jester symbol of the one-hundred-and-four-year-old magazine, into a jester of color.

It wasn't until after college and my move to New York City that most of my best friends were black like me. I wrote about this extensively in "The New Black Aesthetic." I likened my new friends and me to "twins separated at birth—thrilled, soothed, and strengthened in being finally reunited." It was like staying up all night with Ben when we were kids all over again. Before New York, I think I had just resigned myself to never having friends—even friends who were as close as brothers—who would truly understand all aspects of my fractured, culturally mulatto personality. I remember when I told Danny that I was going to write that article, he only half jokingly asked me, "What do you know about black culture?" I realized then how thoroughly I had hidden that part of me from him and Ben. To this day, I think that they see my writings on race and politics as either an affectation or some sort of scam. They knew the raceless Trey and assume that was the only one of me that there ever was. I can't blame them, though. I never ever tried to let them in.

I haven't called either of them in a month or two. It's time.

# WHEN WE WERE FRIENDS: A GEOGRAPHY LESSON

## Bill Ayers

As Alex pushed his dog-eared paperback copy of *Invisible Man* across the table toward me, he lowered his voice: "Here's a present from me to you," he said. "The whole American story in a nutshell." The presentation felt formal, uncharacteristically solemn, some kind of street-level awards ceremony. Thanks, I said, reaching out and taking his hand a bit awkwardly.

Alex Witherspoon and I had been cooking our meals together for months by then, haunting the barbecue joints and local dives together, walking the hard streets of Cleveland's east side, rapping to the people and knocking on doors to "build an interracial movement of the poor." We were mapping the need, but we were also exploring the hope. Were we friends? We were thrust together by our work, our intimacy almost entirely circumstantial, the stuff of shared risk and common experience. We sang together at community gatherings and prayed together at rallies. We picketed and demonstrated and inevitably, I suppose, found ourselves talking about our hopes and our fears, embraced by the quiet and the dark of night. Yes, I thought at the time, we were friends.

Alex was an avid reader—a small pile of books grew and morphed and shrunk like a living thing near his bed, and his back pocket always bulged with a read-in-progress. He'd suggested books to me before, but this exchange, hand-to-hand, was a first. Alex cared about me enough to want to teach me something—about America to be sure, but possibly about himself as well. The whole American story. To me, *Invisible Man* was a gesture of friendship.

When we were friends, we were surely a sight: Alex moved along the street with long, purposeful strides, tall, rail-thin, prominent Afro perched atop a deeply lined face; I, a kind of fresh-faced, white sidekick, wide-eyed and credulous, hurrying to keep up. He was thirty-three-years old, a veteran of the Movement in the South, with a proud record of arrests from the important campaigns; I was twenty and a college dropout, recently arrived from Ann Arbor on a voyage to find the freedom struggle—and myself. We shared an apartment with other organizers, all of us young, idealistic, and filled with the spirit of the civil rights movement in full eruption—when we were friends, I took miracles to be my birthright. Those were the days of wonder, the years of hope. Justice was in reach, I thought, and racism would soon be swept away—a revolution in consciousness, if not in fact, was just beyond the horizon. I felt blessed—sanctified—to be living in this time, of all times, to be present at the awakening: That year I became a volunteer in the army that would take on the American monster, end the American nightmare, and at long last heal the American wound.

We were seeding then what we thought could blossom into a "beloved community" because, as Alex said, "The ghetto's got the richest soil in America to grow a world of peace and freedom." Wondrous strange, but true—he'd laugh his deep, sly laugh, then, his eyes twinkling, and he'd take a pull on his Camel. "America's stark-staring mad, and her best hope is right here in this clarifying wreckage. We're going to make some American magic." The magic began with Alex's wild, unruly way of thinking—*clarifying* wreckage, he'd said, a mind-blowing twist on what had been my one-dimensional gray assumption of need, and need alone—and I loved him for it. In our apartments and in our project houses we shared everything—food and clothes, resources and dreams—and the magic grew stronger. When we were friends, the personal was political and the political personal—we ached to live in a world that could be, but was not yet, and so with one eye on that partially mapped territory of our imaginations, and one eye fixed on the evident east side landscape of hard edges and serious struggle, we soldiered on.

Somewhere in our time together—and I'll pinpoint the moment further on—Alex gave up on the hope of igniting any American magic at all, and he immigrated to West Africa. There had been terrible upheaval by then; there had been ruptures and transformations in him, in me, and in all of us. He didn't call to say goodbye, and I wouldn't have expected it by then. He never wrote from his new land, and I've not seen or heard from him since.

I think of Alex often, picture his hatchet-shaped face split by his encompassing smile, hear his laughing, lilting voice, feel him embrace me and challenge me in a single gesture. Were we friends? I don't know what he would say. But still, Alex left a permanent mark on me, and I see that mark as a gift of friendship.

Some of my best friends—for a long time it felt like a serious sentence; I stood condemned, chained to my desk with an impossible task. "Write about friendship" is the kind of assignment that might take you anywhere, even, if you had the bent, into some dark and treacherous corners. But in the end you can imagine the coffee table book in pastel colors, the panel of authors on *Oprah* repeating all the verities and the hand-me-down stories: true and false friends, friendship tested as fortunes shift, old friends are the best friends. "Write about *interracial* friendships" doesn't entirely preclude those possibilities, because it, too, is a minefield of clichés poised to explode: the against-the-odds love affair, the heroic defiance of bigots on all sides, the betrayal understood too late. I worried, I dawdled. I thought about the ways defying racism—in the world, in relationships—can in a weird way become just another instance of patronization, exotic tourism, self-justification. I thought about all the uninterrogated superiority and smugness that is the baggage and birthright of liberal whites.

But then, as I began to remember Alex, anecdotes and examples of a momentary intimacy, I felt it might be possible that with hard work and a little luck, these some-of-my-best-friends stories might add—implicitly or explicitly—something more: a bit of the history that informs—or deforms—even the most intimate details of our personal lives in America; the power of race as it flows through the prism of the everyday; the complicated dance of individual choice with socially determined structure; the problem of being free *and* fated, fated and free. What happens when the inescapable indictment of being black in America collides with the easy justification of whiteness? How does one walled existence break through to a part of another, and shake hands? How could friendship develop against that brick wall of reality, or why wouldn't it?

I'd come to Cleveland in the spring of 1966 to work as an organizer with the East Side Community Union and to set up a little preschool in a church basement, a predecessor to Head Start. Alex had been a militant with SNCC (Student Nonviolent Coordinating Committee) in the South, and preceded me in Cleveland by a year, home to care for his mother and to help set up the Community Union. I'd left behind a map of my life already drawn, a picture of privilege and access that felt to me not only predictable but uninteresting, flat, and pointless. I yearned for something more vital, more purposeful, and so I arrived in Cleveland an exile. We were from different places, headed to different places, but for one dazzling moment, our paths intersected.

The Movement was shifting away from attacks on the *legal* barriers to integration, mostly in retreat by then. We organized, instead, around *de facto* segregation and issues of economic justice; we intended to build an unstoppable force of poor people in the big cities of the North, who, we thought, would not only improve their own lives, but would along the way turn the planet upside down. We borrowed inspiration and songs from the humanizing energy of the southern Movement, but we were drawing new lines and plowing new ground in these concrete ghetto streets. "Oh Freedom, Oh Freedom."

Alex knew *Invisible Man* almost by heart, and we talked about it off and on for days, laughing at some scenes, practically crying at others. I wasn't a complete innocent—I'd read Richard Wright and James Baldwin—but Ellison opened another window onto a wider field.

"I am an invisible man," he begins. "I am invisible, understand, simply because people refuse to see me . . ." The horror of being alive but flailing unseen in the void, the frightful struggle against powerful forces actively determined to erase your humanity and subjectivity, to turn you into an object, a thing: "[T]hey see only my surroundings, themselves, or figments of their imagination—indeed, everything and anything except me." The anguished personal cry that refuses to be swallowed up in the vacuum felt to me like a universal description true of each of us.

One morning, as we sipped coffee and munched eggs and toast at a diner, still talking about Ellison, Alex surprised me. "We haven't even mentioned yet the most important line in the book," he said in what seems now like a running tutorial. "And it's right up front in the prologue." I didn't know what he meant. "Remember the part where the preacher takes as his text the 'Blackness of Blackness,' " he said. "And he chants out 'black is . . . an' black ain't'? When I first read that I practically stopped breathing." He looked at me hard for a moment. Why? I asked. "I mean, that's it: Black is . . . an' black ain't. The whole thing—race itself, man—it's a joke, but you can't laugh . . . It's a fantastic joke, and it's killing us—all of us in America." *Invisible Man* was the atlas, and Alex, to me the most visible of men, the tutor. To say I admired Alex would miss a lot. I idolized him.

Our apartment was a third-floor walk-up in an anonymous brick building on Lakeview Avenue, one of a long line of shabby buildings slouching toward the street as far as the eye could see. The poverty struck me at first like a fist—I'd never seen anything like it, even though I'd read about it in books by then, and seen many, many pictures of poor people in haunt- ingly beautiful photographs. But those anaesthetizing images conveyed nothing of the smell of hardship or the taste of want, the enveloping feel of need. In Cleveland, I saw for the first time what it was to be broke, not just waiting for a check; and what it was to be hungry, not just ready for lunch.

The organizers—eight of us—read and studied together, and sometimes Alex would lead a more formal session of polit- ical education. Books were part of our lives, and the books we sought were those that might be wielded as weapons in the struggle—*The Fire Next Time, The Wretched of the Earth*. When we were young, we were hungry for affirmation and for any formulation that might clarify, amplify, or point us toward effective action. We wanted charts and maps. I remember Alex reading Kenneth Clark aloud one evening: "the dark ghetto's invisible walls have been erected by the white society . . . to confine those who have no power and to perpetuate their pow- erlessness [in] social, political, educational, and—above all— economic colonies."

Alex nodded his head as he read. "Lakeview and Hough didn't just happen," he said. "This neighborhood's an actual colony, its colonial status enforced with all the power of law and money, and with violence or the threat of violence when peaceful means fail." A colony—it seemed to describe all that we surveyed there, and a lightbulb went on for me. Alex argued that racism as bigotry was built upon the hard ground of race as a convenient invention for colonization and exploitation. My learning landscape opened and widened a bit.

Knots of men collected on corners and in the vacant lot next to our building, smoking, passing a bottle or a skinny joint. They were unemployed or underemployed, always waiting it seemed, inmates in some camp. The colonized, Alex would say. Ordinary folks—they paid their taxes, loved their children, and put their pants on one leg at a time just like you and me— assigned to this artificial city-within-a-city, this colony as Alex now always called our community, and why? "They hold no cur- rency," Alex said. "They lack funds, influence, access to power, and for that, they're trapped." The immense panorama of waste and cruelty was overwhelming; our everyday work organizing rent strikes or community speak outs, petition campaigns or political rallies, was designed at root to help our neighbors col- lectively resist the casual disregard of their own humanity.

On our corner, a group of street characters, all fixtures on our block, well known, reliable, and oddly reassuring, gathered for early morning parleys—part news bulletin, part scandal sheet, part debate, part bull session, part ongoing dominoes tournament. Eddie Robbins was called Thunderbird; James Thompson was Little Bit; Willie Jones was now Ismael Akbar, father of three little girls with their own recent name changes—they were now Mali, Kenya, and Ghana. Alex, of course, saw this as prime organizing turf, and soon the men allowed me in, too; I hung out there, paying for my admission by being the first schoolteacher any of them knew who lived right there on the block with them, and because Akbar, who believed that all white people are devils, said that nevertheless I was a good teacher for his girls.

I was perhaps a bit too eager to please, and certainly exhilarated to be an exception to the white-people-are-devils construct. I read a deflating essay by Amiri Baraka around this time defending the white-people-as-devils thesis, pointing out all the ways whites are willfully, defensively ignorant even as they concretely benefit from the hierarchy of race. Working himself into a lather on the subject, Baraka busts out with, "I mean *all* white people are devils, even Dave Debusschere." If the great *Knicks* forward is a devil, I thought, how much could I hope for myself?

Inside myself, a rift already well under way was deepening: Skeptical of religious appeals, suspicious of most universals, I nonetheless thought that most white people were indeed devils, or that they acted in all kinds of devilish ways. As I appraised America through the looking glass, with the lens of the ghetto, the colony, it didn't take long for my world to flip on its head.

Why is it, Akbar asked one day, that this neighborhood is full of Washingtons, Lincolns, and Franklin Roosevelts?

True, Alex said. And I've never seen a white baby named Lumumba.

There was a whole education to be had on the corner: You hear Henry Allen beating up on that gal's been staying with him?

Yeah, it got plenty loud about midnight.

And when she was shrieking there at the end, and he threw her out the window?

Man, I saw her fall, don't know how she lived.

Yeah, and the cops was here in thirty minutes, ambulance took a hour, she coulda died.

Black people don't mean a thing to them, man. Whenever you want them, you can't get them for a prayer, but when you don't want them, man, they're *everywhere*.

The buzz was sometimes complaining, sometimes boasting, sometimes bitter, always shot through with a quick line of laughter. The subject of white folks was never far away.

I like all the reading going on at your school, Bill, Akbar began one morning. But you should weed out some of those books. Some are silly, some absolutely racist.

Racist?

That Dr. Seuss, he spit out. He travels around the world collecting specimens for a zoo, and you see how he treats all the brothers? White, white, white. And silly.

Or Curious George, Alex chimed in. The man in the yellow hat goes to Africa and kidnaps a cute little monkey, brings him back in a cage on a ship, and they live happily ever after.

Exactly! said Akbar. Racist to the bone!

Man, Akbar said on another day. You see what they doing now? They talking about making kayaking and synchronized swimming Olympic events. Everybody knows black people don't like the water. Just another racist scheme to keep us from those medals.

Yea, man, replied Little Bit. You right. Why don't those white people make double-dutch jump rope an Olympic event?

Exactly, and I'll tell you why. Akbar again. Because Mali and Kenya and Ghana'd be up there on that stand, little black angels giving a black eye to the festival of whiteness.

Pride and rebellion, excess and self-delusion, always laughter.

Alex was a public character and a street philosopher like the others, and a smart organizer, to boot. The people with the problems, he often said, are also the ones with the solutions. He had an extensive knowledge of the history of race science, the eugenics movement, the slave trade, and the Holocaust in Europe. It's all a fantastic joke, he insisted again. In the service of inequality. If you're in favor of justice, you've got to be against race, period.

I'm not so sure, Akbar said now. I've been black all my life, and I'm finally black and proud, so don't snatch that from me just yet.

Okay, Alex allowed. Be black and proud for now, but let's change this monster system so we can all be human and happy.


"What color am I?" Alex asked me once as he and I walked down the street.

"You're black," I said, surprised.

"Why so insistent?"

"I'm not insistent. I'm just assuming."

"So you assume I'm black, and society confirms your assumption with a whole catalog of assumptions of its own, and so it becomes what? A fact, like the 'fact' that you're white . . . But you know, you've got a matriarch from Ethiopia way back somewhere. And look at me—I'm dark, but I'm not black."

"True, you're brown."

"I have a white grandmother and a white great grandfather. How much white I got to have to qualify?"

"To qualify for what?"

"For membership in the country club of the fully human."

Alex made sense. Before I knew him, race was fixed for me—the secure, received wisdom of American common sense—but by the time he was through, race had been queered up in my head. It was real—I could *see* it, could benefit or suffer from it—and it was false—the perverse invention of some mad genius. "Man," he would say some days before bed. "Another hard day in the war to make white Americans better people." We laughed together, but I held an impossible hope: that his comment was somehow aimed at others, never at me.

We worked hard to become part of our community in order to resist its reduction to a colony. We projected a map of possibility. I listened to what people said, and was as respectful as I knew how to be to my new neighbors. We all wanted to become good citizens of our block. "Don't make a big thing of it," Alex said to me one morning. "But always pick up the litter on your way to the bus stop."

When we were friends, our innocence exposed us and left us vulnerable on occasion, but more often it protected us—I think God does look after babies and fools. We knocked on doors, talked around kitchen tables, hung out on stoops, and went to picnics in the park. I was an identifiable outsider, of course, living there by choice, not necessity, but I went earnestly door-to-door, trying to engage people in conversations that might reveal the obstacles they faced in their lives, and in naming those barriers, creating the possibility of coming together with others to chart a struggle for repair. I'm sure some people were suspicious or mistrustful, and why shouldn't they be? Who were these outsiders, these agitators? Who was this white boy? But what struck me then, and touches me even now, was how many folks readily embraced me, took me into their homes, their families, their lives. While my motives and ambitions might never be fully sorted out, no one questioned my humanity, no one doubted the humanizing potential of the Movement, and most people greeted me with abundant faith and extraordinary goodwill.

When Alex had first knocked on Dorothea Hill's door, she opened with a big welcoming smile. "Oh, you're the civil rights kids from down the block," she'd said. "I've been waiting for you. Come on in." We talked long into the night about children, welfare, schools, and crime, all the problems of life in the neighborhood. Later when I asked Mrs. Hill why she'd told Alex she'd been waiting for us, she laughed and said, "I saw the Movement on television for years fighting for justice; as poor as I am, I figured after a while it would have to reach my door."

Dorothea Hill had grown up on the block and was now raising her own children there. She was active in her church and

PTA, and she was the person others looked to for guidance and help. When a child was hit by a car on Lakeview Avenue, it was Mrs. Hill who called a meeting in her living room to press the city to install a stop light; when a back-to-school welfare allowance was cut, Mrs. Hill organized the protest; when a rat bit a youngster while she slept in her apartment, Dorothea thought up the dramatic tactic of taking dead rats with us downtown to the demonstration and piling them on the front steps. Get the rats out of Lakeview and city hall, Mrs. Hill chanted.

Mrs. Hill opened meetings with devotions, part prayer, part politics: Thank you Lord for Your many blessings, for Your mercy, and please, Lord, help us out on this demonstration next week. Then we sang songs—"May the Circle Be Unbroken," "This Little Light of Mine"—to bring us together as a group, reminding us of our common purpose, and making us all feel a little stronger. When she began to set the agenda, Mrs. Hill would always interject her own words of wisdom: "Tonight we'll be talking about welfare rights and the Welfare Work Book we'll be publishing soon; now remember, just because you're poor and on welfare doesn't mean you're not a citizen, and citizens have rights."

Alex and I organized half a dozen neighbors to work on an action-research project with us. We bought five pounds of hamburger from the supermarket on our street, and then traveled all over the area buying five pounds of hamburger from every branch we could find on different days—other black neighborhoods, a poor white community, working-class and wealthy suburbs. We cooked up the meat under controlled conditions—in Dorothea's kitchen in her big, black, cast-iron frying pan over medium heat—while we all watched. When we poured off the grease, bingo: The hamburger sold in the black neighborhoods was twice as fatty as that sold in Shaker Heights; the white burger always leaner than the black burger. After carefully charting our findings in the earnest pose of researchers, Dorothea added tomato paste and beans and we all joined in to eat the research results—fat and lean—over fluffy white rice. Those meals were like an awards banquet without the stiff formality—we laughed and cheered and joked and heard a few spontaneous congratulatory speeches; Dorothea insisted that everyone eat and eat and eat; and Alex dispensed the lessons. He was awesome at these moments, funny, charming, at once self-mocking and serious: If we keep this up, we'll have justice in the meat departments of the world in just a few hundred years, he'd say, and everyone would bust out laughing. We imagined greater victories just ahead.

When we were friends the world was in flames—Vietnam, Santo Domingo, Sharpesville—it reeled in agony and despair, and still most Americans seemed to be sleepwalking through the whole thing, unaware, uninvolved, disengaged. In the middle of that summer, we were swept along by something red and violent in our own backyard—an urban uprising to some, a rebellion; and to others, black anarchy and a ghetto riot.

Stories rushed up the street faster than fire: Cops on Superior Street beat a woman on her way to church, and on St. Clair a cop shot a boy point-blank and called him "nigger." But on Euclid, two cop cars were burned to a crisp, a bank was trashed, and money was blowing in great gusts down the street.

True or not, each story was embraced and passed along, each somehow true simply because it was believed.

The strange thing was to live in an atmosphere simultaneously terrifying and deeply energizing. The mood was festive one minute, a giant community picnic, everyone laughing and sharing and handing things around, and the next minute the sound of shots fired from somewhere, or the sight of flames leaping suddenly to life, and we would all turn and scatter. One afternoon, I saw thirty or forty people—young and old, men and women, the respectable as well as the neighborhood characters—pulling together to tear a grate off the large plate-glass window of the supermarket. No one urged caution, and no one objected. That night, Donald Hall, a kid who worked with the Community Union but would, in a year, join a black nationalist group and change his name to Jamal Daoud, showed up at our apartment, singed and smoky, took a shower, and left with fresh clothes from Alex. "People are fed up," Alex said to me flatly. "We've been dispossessed so long, maybe taking back isn't so bad." Night after night, day after day, each majestic scene was so terrible and so unexpected that no built environment would ever again stand innocently fixed in my mind—every human topography became temporary.

The project house became our command post and community center—Dorothea and half a dozen others took turns distributing food and coffee and medicine to a large crowd every morning, and I ran a regular ambulance service to the emergency room in my beat-up Oldsmobile. Returning from the hospital one night after curfew, Alex and I were surprised at a checkpoint on Lakeview Avenue, stopped at gunpoint, spread-eagled on the pavement, searched, and released, but not before a whole rash of questions about what a white guy was doing with a black guy on Lakeview Avenue in the middle of all this. I saw the ordinary bond of racial solidarity smashed on the ground there: I was with Alex; I was not with them. The baby-faced Ohio National Guardsman, a white boy who'd probably been pumping gas in Akron the day before, searched me, sweating and breathing heavily, looking wide-eyed and terrified. I was terrified, too, and I felt unhinged. Alex and I didn't dwell on it—we weren't actually hurt, and, anyway, things were bad everywhere.

Stokely Carmichael, who had raised the banner of Black Power on a march in Mississippi that summer of 1967, spoke to hundreds of people at a church down the street from the Community Union a few weeks later—we can't wait for white people to decide whether we're worthy of our freedom, he said. We must *take* our freedom. We can't allow others to do for us. We must *do* for ourselves. We can't accept white standards of beauty or intelligence. We must *rid* ourselves of self-hatred. This much is crystal clear, he said. We're one hundred percent human, and like other humans, we need the power to run our own lives. We're black, and we want power. Black; power. Black Power. The church vibrated with the excited chant, and I remember a boy of fourteen or fifteen with a huge smile racing up and down the aisles with his fist pumping, inciting us to be louder. I was one of maybe a half-dozen whites sprinkled through the jammed and pulsing crowd, and I chanted along with the rest.

112

Stokely's words were interpreted by Movement people again and again over the next months to mean that I should get out of the way and organize "my own people." It felt both necessary and false. Necessary because I knew by then that the problem of racism was in fact a problem of white people. False because they didn't feel in any way like "my own people."

My allegiances and nonallegiances deepened and settled in that year—I would stand with Dorothea or Alex against the complacent or the mighty, or both at once. With privilege and oppression organized along a strict hierarchy of race, I wanted to claim my allegiance to humanity, to somehow become enemy or exile—not to deny the racial reality, but to refuse its seductions. I wanted to interrupt the common sense of race, to side with the people of the world against the small but power- ful group of dangerous men determined to dominate. Easier said, of course, than done.

Before that summer, we began each meeting with a song, but after all that had happened, whenever we opened our mouths to sing, it seemed we could only scream. The apocalypse was upon us, the serial assassination of black leaders in America linked somehow in our minds to Lumumba's and to the thou- sands of made-in-America murders in Vietnam every day. The air was acrid in our throats, and we felt the approach of a police state. We steeled ourselves. Alex began to spend more time away from the project, to sleep away from our apartment, and to keep his own counsel. I missed his radiance mostly, but I was consumed with my own changes, and with the more serious demands of a more intense time. There was less and less talk of our beloved community, and more and more of self-determination, anticolonial struggle, revolution. Alex had a foot in both territories for a time, but then he slipped away, not an invisible man, but a man without a country. I remembered James Baldwin's assertion that a black man's attitude is designed to "rob the white man of the jewel of his naïvete, or else to make it cost him dear." Alex had tried the former, and now, I thought, he'd exact a cost. Alex was a revolutionary, and the stakes were rising.

Were we friends? I ask myself, and more than thirty-five years later, the question startles me. There was a shared purpose in our relationship, to be sure—we were building a movement to change the world. We were earnest, driven, flying on a freedom high fueled by action and hope and then more action. I would have said at the time that, yes, we were friends, but now I'm not so sure.

Alex criticized me freely and often, instructed me and corrected me. It never would have occurred to me to answer in kind. I was young, for one thing, and I was stretching. I can think of a dozen practical gifts and lessons Alex bestowed on me—*Invisible Man* and much more—but I can't think of a thing I gave to him. Were we friends? If friendship asks reciprocity, if a friend finds a way to be loyal but critical, supportive but demanding, then Alex *was* my friend, and perhaps I failed the core requirements of friendship in return.

Of course, there are as many ways to be friends as there are stars in the sky. The map of our friendship included roads under construction, projects not completed, borders and boundaries and breakthroughs, and then new walls. When we were friends, our relationship seemed at once the most natural thing in the world and a complete aberration. We were thrust together in common cause against a hard and resistant world, breaking barriers to inhabit uncharted territory. Ours was an intimacy of action, as good as any other perhaps.

But in the large, dynamic republic of friendship, there are all kinds: false friendships and failed friendships, superficial friendships and partial friendships, male bonding and sisterhood is powerful, momentary encounters and lifelong intimacies. Alex and I did things together—someone once called this "friends in spots"—and surely, like men in combat or on the gridiron, there was some posture and a swagger in the room when we were together. But what occurred between us transported me from one territory to another, across ocean and sky to a new continent. Ours was a brief friendship—surely the kind of intimacy that lasts eluded the two of us—but with a depth and a heft that's never left me. I count our friendship as partial, but real.

Soon the Black Panthers, the Black Liberation Army, and the Republic of New Africa would explode onto the scene, George Jackson and the Attica Brothers and Fred Hampton would be assassinated, and I would set off on the run for over a decade, charged with conspiracy to cross state lines to incite riots and attack government property. Alex had been a generous teacher—he established a standard of honesty, integrity, and courage for me to aspire to, and he set a pattern that has lasted my whole life—I still seek out a mentor or a tutor even now, wherever I am. When it's my turn to be the teacher, I remember Alex on the corner—you have to be willing to listen and learn because people are always the experts on their own lives, he'd say, but at the same time, you have to be willing to tell the whole truth as you see it.

Ralph Ellison writes, ". . . my world has become one of infinite possibilities. What a phrase—still it's a good phrase and a good view of life, and a man shouldn't accept any other; that much I've learned underground. Until some gang succeeds in putting the world in a straitjacket, its definition is possibility. Step outside the narrow borders of what men call reality and you step into chaos . . . or imagination."

When we were young, stepping outside the narrow borders of received reality was our creed. We imagined that another world was possible. Somewhere I picture Alex now: stepping out, living fully inside the vortex.

# IN MY HEART
# IS A DARKNESS

## Michelle Cliff

I

The most important interracial relationship I have is with myself. I move through the landscape a double agent, where I listen and learn.

On a plane on the way to Houston, I overhear a conversation between two men. Actually, it's more of a monologue. The speaker is American, holding forth to a European about Texas history: Sam Houston, Santa Ana, the Battle of San Jacinto.

Houston's troops—he says—killed "six hundred goddamn Mexicans." The Texans were able to accomplish this because the Mexicans were taking a siesta (caught napping) and Santa Ana was "fucking this little mulatto gal from one of the plantations."

The "little mulatto gal became known as the yellow rose of Texas."

This little mulatto gal adds that bit of lore to her store of a million items. In the words of Bessie Head (another little mulatto gal): I am the "collector of such treasures."

From *The Hornes*:

> *Lena began the civil rights decade with a well-aimed
> missile to a bigot's head—not a nonviolent protest . . .
> Lena overheard a waiter telling a boorish drunk that he
> would be with him in a minute, as soon as he'd finished
> "serving Lena Horne." But the drunk wanted instant
> service. "Where is Lena Horne, anyway?" the drunk wanted
> to know. "She's just another nigger," he added. At that
> point Lena stood up and said, "Here I am, you bastard!
> Here's the nigger you couldn't see," and proceeded to hurl a
> large glass ashtray at the man's head.* *

You go, girl.

Glenn Ligon at the Carnegie Museum of Art in Pittsburgh:

"We are the ink that gives the white page a meaning."
Repeated and repeated as the letters darken the white canvas.
Do whites rely on blacks for a sense of being. Why does the
black image exist in the white mind.

Across the town at Warhol:

Without Sanctuary: a pictorial reliquary. Repetitiveness of
images: rope, elongated bodies, bowed head. Still bodies
against excited spectators. The only movement the activity of
the mob. The effect is numbing. What of the struggle before.
The pleas for mercy. The dragging through the dirt. Last words:
pleas, fury. But these are the stuff of souvenir—what wants to
be remembered. Stillness, silence is essential not to rattle the
white imagination.

---

* *Gail Lumet Buckley*, The Hornes (New York: Knopf, 1986), p. 242.

I have not failed to be disappointed (with very few exceptions) in my relationships with white people—American and European. Very few of my best friends are white. I learned at an early age to protect myself. I have learned over the years that most white people have internalized supremacist values, taken their skin privilege for granted. That many of the well-meaning among them fall into the Schweitzerian category: Albert Schweitzer remarking that yes, the African was his brother, albeit his younger brother. The elder European brother striding through his medical colony, while strains of Bach fall upon native ears. Humanitarian, perhaps, but with a smidge of Kurtz.

Others express their solidarity differently: In Kentucky once at a women writers' conference, I attended a reading by Sonia Sanchez. As she read her prose poem, "Norma,"* about the destruction of brilliance in a young black woman, I found myself weeping, out of control. Later, a white woman approached me and said she had seen my response to the poem and wanted to come over and comfort me, but "I was afraid you'd kill me."

I gave the keynote at a conference several years ago; the focus of the conference was the writing of the white American antiracist Lillian Smith, a volume of which I had edited in the late seventies. On the final day, at the final panel, a dapper little white Southern gentleman who had known Miss Lillian, and had witnessed her efforts to bring the races together in her home in northern Georgia, raised his hand and inquired: Why was the use of the word *nigger* off limits for whites? My good-

---

\* *In* Homegirls & Handgrenades *(New York: Thunder's Mouth Press, 1984), p. 19 ff.*

ness, in Miss Lillian's own living room, he had heard Eslanda Robeson refer to her husband as "My Nigger Paul" (he repeated this three times)—if she could do that, then what was wrong with this dapper little man doing likewise? I waited for the chair of the panel, a white woman, to speak, but she appeared frozen, and I presumed to address the question. I asked the little man if he did not understand the difference between Eslanda Robeson's use of the word and his own desire. I pressed: Why did he want the privilege of the utterance? The chair defrosted, addressing the little man: "I think what Michelle is trying to say . . ."

Sometimes it's best to keep one's distance, play the fool, the trickster, Anansi, the crafty spider—the Signifying Monkey—

## I I

### TEN SIMPLE TESTS

#### (EARLY DETECTION MAY SAVE YOUR ASS)

**1. You repeat the African-American legend that Ava Gardner was a black woman passing for white.**

The recipient of this news may react with disbelief.

What about Linda Darnell? Dorothy Lamour? Joseph
   Cotten?

You abandon African-American legend and dig in:
   Cary Grant? Marlon Brando? Marilyn Monroe?
   Ingrid Bergman?

You wait for: What are you talking about? Are you
   crazy? Nuts? Fucking with me?

Why on earth should it matter?

**2. You are asked at a dinner party about your background.**

You respond that your great-plus-five grandfather
on your father's side was the youngest son of a
British earl, and since he could not inherit the
family estate, immigrated to Jamaica to seek his
fortune.

"Ahhh . . ."

You continue that the ancestors on your mother's side
hailed from Africa.

"Ohhh . . ."


**3. Allow how you once went through a village north of
Boston and poured buckets of white paint over the lawn
jockeys in front of the country club in the dead of night.
Whitefacing private property. "Weren't you afraid you'd
get caught?" Do they not realize the irresistibility of
such an act?**

Does anyone raise the historicity of the lawn jockey:
shining a light for General Washington?

While we're on the subject of defacing, ask the gathered company how many realized that the blacks in
*Birth of a Nation* were played by white actors in
blackface.

Note their reaction to the news.

What do they think about Bert Williams applying
burnt cork to his face?


**4. Invent a board game: the search for Michael Jackson's nose.
Roll the dice and advance your counter from Gary, Indiana,
and a little round-faced black boy, to Neverland, California,**

and a Peter Pan incarnadine (a word which means, according to Webster's, "pink, flesh-colored"). Are the other players able to see the (black) humor embedded in the self-hatred? Or is the man with the plasticine face only pitied?

5. Discuss Toni Morrison. Tell them that when you read *The Bluest Eye* you want to put your hand into the book and draw out Pecola Breedlove and hold her and rock her and tell her you will make everything right for her. And then you weep because it is too late. And you have the blues.

> The [Blues]t Eye
> [Blues]tone road  [Bluest]one  Beloved  Be loved
> When Morrison's awarded the Nobel Prize, what's the
>   buzz at a New York cocktail party?

6. Image from 1985: Old man in Philadelphia on the six o'clock news: His five-hundred-disc jazz collection melted by a percussion grenade employed to destroy MOVE. Does the assembled company know about MOVE? About John African? What do they think of it? Have they read the work of John Edgar Wideman? "Oh, yes, *Brothers & Keepers.* The one about his brother in prison for murder." Right.

7. Mention at a conference that Heathcliff was a black man and gauge the response. Remind the audience of the signals Emily Brontë sends. Suggest the source of Heathcliff's fury—not romantic rejection but the trading in human souls (his people) during his three-year absence from Wuthering

Heights. Bring it home with the fact that the actual house in which the novel is based was the homestead of a slave trader. Why does Mr. Earnshaw travel to Liverpool to attend to business? Why not Bradford, Leeds?

> Remind them further—while we're on the Brontës—
> that the madwoman in the attic was actually
> the mad black woman in the attic. Confined.
> Furious.

8. Compare O. J. Simpson, Wilt Chamberlain, Mapplethorpe's headless **Man in Polyester Suit.** Recite the text from Glenn Ligon's **Mudbone (Liar),** 1993.

> *Niggers had the biggest dicks in the world, and they were trying to find a place where they could have they contest. And they wasn't no freak, they didn't want everybody looking. So they walking around looking for a secret place. So they walked across the Golden Gate Bridge and the nigger seen the water and made him wanna piss. One said, "Man, I got to take a leak." And he pulled his things out and was pissing. Other nigger pulled his out, took a piss.*
>
> *One nigger said, "Goddamn, this water cold!"*
> *The other nigger say, "Yeah, and it's deep too!"*\*

Do they weep for Emmett Till in his watery grave? Will they be able to connect the absurd with the horror?

---

\* *In* Black Male, *ed. Thelma Golden (New York: Whitney Museum of American Art, 1994), p. 57.*

Do they understand what Dany Laferrière means when he says: "You're not born black, you get that way?"[*]

9. **The Venus Hottentot. Dorothy Dandridge. Billie Holiday. What elements of connection can the assembled company name between these three? How is Josephine Baker related to these three? How does she diverge? Is it racist to refer to La Bakaire as the "Signifying Monkey?" What do you think of her "Rainbow Tribe"?**

10. **What was the Red Summer of 1919? When and why did Frederick Douglass and Sojourner Truth have the following exchange:**

S: Frederick! Is God dead?
F: No, God is not dead and therefore slavery must end in blood.

What do they think of John Brown? Remind them of Lorraine Hansberry's longing that the American liberal become the American radical. What's the hold-up?

### III

So much for lightheartedness. Trickery. The Signifying Monkey signs off.

For me, friendship is the most precious bond between two

---

[*]*Dany Laferrière*, How to Make Love to a Negro *(Toronto: Coach House Press, 1987)*, *p. 117.*

individuals. The basis of this bond is trust. Nothing can destroy the trust I place in another human being more than my realization that the racism he or she has imbibed through his or her place in society as a white citizen is very much alive and well; with this, trust is irrevocably breached. This has happened in my life too many times to recount, and so I approach friendship with a white person with more than a dash of skepticism. But my situation is a peculiar one. As a light-skinned un-American—Afro Saxon—I have been accused of wanting to be black. I have been told time and again that I don't look like a real Jamaican, nor do I speak like one, nor are my cultural references located solely in the Caribbean. All that means is the template cut by the white imagination—European or American—cannot accommodate my appearance, speech pattern, or intellect as a West Indian. And when the white imagination is disrupted by matters of race, it becomes agitated. Its sense of neatness is disturbed. When the Other appears to be the One. Apocalypso.

Like Walcott's "fortunate traveler," I may become homeless. To that I would reply that the sea is my home, as are the volcanoes which create the islands, erupting from the sea.

## IV

Intimacy suffers. I have practiced my own version of safe sex. Protecting myself with language, wit. This lends a certain lack of spontaneity to a private life, but at least I don't hear remarks about the "neat" positions I can achieve beneath the limbo pole. The system, needless to say, is not foolproof.

## V

The theme of interraciality—of heritage and relationship— exists throughout my work. In my novels, the forging of friend- ship across lines of race and class—Clare and Zoe in *Abeng*; Clare and Harry/Harriet in *No Telephone to Heaven*; Mary Ellen Pleasant and John Brown in *Free Enterprise*—comprise politi- cal acts.

In the latter two novels, these friendships, hard-won— between a light-skinned woman and a black man and an African-American woman and a white American man—move from the privacy of relationships into public acts of insurrec- tion. Each individual motivated by the *agape* celebrated by Che Guevara.

I see these friendships as existing on a continuum: culmi- nating in the truly revolutionary connection between Mary Ellen Pleasant and John Brown. Their love for each other— which is based in history—is an act of revolution. When they put this love into action[*] it informs their revolutionary mission—nothing more or less than the overthrow of the slave- holding states and the release from bondage of the many thou- sands.

---

[*] Elizabeth Bishop, "Chemin de Fer" (*The Complete Poems* [New York: Farrar, Straus & Giroux, 1969]):

*"Love should be put into action!"*
*screamed the old hermit.*
*Across the pond an echo*
*Tried and tried to confirm it.*

126

*In the end we were two people with love for each other.*
*It was that simple. That much of a wonder. And while I*
*did not agree with J.B.'s vision of the dark-skinned future,*
*I never for a minute distrusted his love.*

*I have grown so weary of the interrupted conversations.*
*That is what death is. It breaks off words between people. It*
*leaves you with a longing for one last talk, or two, or three.*
*A chance to say, "I do love you. I always will."*

*I was down South when I heard they hanged him. I*
*spent the day, head down, left foot dragging, immersed in*
*memory. Can you hear me? I said aloud.*

*When he was captured there was a piece of paper in*
*his pocket, with my words on it. "The axe is laid at the*
*foot of the tree. When the first blow is struck, there will*
*be more money to help."*

*Not much of a farewell, but at least a promise.*[*]

Questions must be asked: Why is this friendship a historical
secret? Why has John Brown been pictured a madman,
scoundrel, or worse? Why has Mary Ellen Pleasant disappeared?

I assure the reader I did not make this friendship up. When
I visited Mary Ellen Pleasant's grave in Napa and saw her
epitaph—chosen by her—it rocked me for the exceptional possibilities it represented and I quoted it twice in *Free Enterprise*;
once at the very end—

> *she . . . would one day abide in Napa, overwhelmed by*
> *a white oleander, arched by the thorns and fruit of a wild*

---

[*] *Michelle Cliff,* Free Enterprise *(New York: Dutton, 1993), p. 151.*

*blackberry bush, each growing from her. The berries in
season staining the white marble of her gravestone, the
black juice running into the letters she chose,*

SHE WAS A FRIEND OF JOHN BROWN[*]

No more, no less. Such friendship is a triumph of imagination—on every level an act of liberation.

[*]*Cliff,* Free Enterprise, *p. 213.*

# SECRET COLORS

## David Mura

### I

For many years I wanted to be white. I worshipped white heroes on television, chose Paladin over his Chinese messenger, the Cartwrights over Hop Sing, the Green Hornet over Kato; identified with John Wayne shooting the Japs, with Richard Widmark wiping out the Koreans. The racial component of these identifications never came up. They seemed perfectly natural.

When younger I did have Japanese-American friends, especially when we lived in the city, but after we moved to the suburbs, I gradually began to move away from the two Japanese-American brothers in the neighborhood and avoided any other friendships with other Asian Americans. The one other Japanese-American boy in my classes was a definite nerd; so was the one Chinese-American boy. Who would want to be associated with them? Other than Asians, there were no other people of color at my schools. In my teens, some fellow students expected me to look toward the few Asian-American girls at our school. I resented this and desired just the opposite. It seemed to me a compliment when white friends would say, "I think of you, David, just like a white person." That was exactly how I wanted them to think of me—as if there were no differences between us.

Given those early exchanges, I could say, Yes, interracial friendships with whites are possible. Certainly they are possible if the person of color thinks of himself as white or desires to be thought of as white—that is, if the person of color forces from his consciousness the differences in his experience of race or how he might view himself differently from his white friend. Such friendships are also possible if race is never discussed as part of the relationship (some interracial marriages even function in this way). In such instances, the person of color might be aware of differences and difficulties due to racial issues, but remains silent about them. Instead, the person of color suppresses his true feelings and presents a version of himself he thinks will please, or at least not trouble, the white friend.

Under such conditions, friendship is possible. But we might ask then: What kind of friendship is that?

Furthermore, what happens if the person of color begins to become conscious of his identity in a way that takes into account his experiences of race?

Finally, how are interracial friendships between people of color different from those between people of color and whites?

These, perhaps, are more difficult and revealing questions than simply whether interracial friendships are possible.

To explain my perspective on these questions, let me give some biographical context.

In the early eighties, after a failed stint in graduate school, I became part of the Twin Cities literary scene. At that time, many of my friends who were artists went into therapy and began dealing with the problems of addiction and abusive family systems. Feminist critiques of the patriarchy, of pornography, of sexual

roles, figured prominently in our discussions. These friends supported me through my questioning of my family, my investiga-
tions into my sexuality, my own unexamined rage and depression.
I could share with them intimate secrets about my sexual behavior, such as my infidelities in my relationship with my girlfriend.
They helped me climb out of a deep cavern of shame, which
seemed to echo the world of my childhood. We discussed addic-
tions in our families, the craziness or inscrutability or remoteness
or abuses of our parents. We supported one another in creating a
"family of choice" to replace our "biological family."

At the same time, I was learning what it was to be a poet, a
writer, in this country. This role included not just discussions on
the "deep image" or the relevance of meter and rhyme or the
feminist poetics of Adrienne Rich. There was also a community
we felt we were all building, a new way of supporting writers
through an arts organization like The Loft in the Twin Cities.
Some of us were exploring a new way of teaching writing that
relied more on process and the techniques of therapeutic questioning, rather than simply striking a line here or rearranging a
phrase there. There were questions of whether we wanted to
teach at a university or not. Though even as we questioned the
"academic poet," many of us saw such jobs as enviable positions, the just reward for success as a writer. There was also a
lifestyle that seemed to seek an existence of quiet solitude and
work; whether in summers in a cabin at the North Shore of
Lake Superior or within the everyday life in the city, one tried to
arrange one's life and its surrounding objects so that they were
infused with a sense of beauty and poetry—not an ostentatious,
opulent, upper-class style, but a lyrical bohemianism that probably dated back to some notion of Paris in the twenties. (Not

that this lifestyle was always affordable to every one of us, only that it shaped our desires.)

What is obvious to me now is that my friends and community, the artists and writers I admired, were all white. Occasionally, circumstances would make me aware of myself as a single Asian American in one of the whitest cities in this country, yet more often than not, the issues of race rarely crossed my mind. When an anthology of Minnesota writers came out and there were no black or Hispanic or Native-American writers in the anthology, I did not really think of myself as a token person of color. Instead, my presence in the anthology simply affirmed my position as one of the top poets in the state. One of the editors was a close friend, and when someone wrote to complain of the lack of writers of color, I supported my friend's editorial decisions. Surely, he wasn't a racist; he had struggled over the editing process, and he had chosen to exclude his own work. Part of me agreed with him that there just weren't any other really good poets of color in the state. Look at the demographics, I thought. And the poems I had seen by a few of the black writers, well, they were just flat. They lacked technique.

You see, I saw myself as a good liberal and believed that my friends were good liberals. We were for equality. We were also for literature of quality. If, when we gathered at parties or literary events, I was the only person of color in the room, that didn't say anything about me or my white friends.

A few years passed. On a warm spring day in the late eighties, I went walking with a white friend, let's call her Cathy, through the streets of St. Paul. This friend was a fellow poet, someone who had read a poem at my wedding. We had worked together in the "Writers in the Schools" program. We were close in age, and, in many ways, close in politics, literary interests, sensibility. We had shared our intimate experiences with therapy, with rummaging through the closets of our dysfunctional family systems. We both grew up in middle-class white suburbs. She was blond and big boned, her ethnic group Scandinavian like many Minnesotans, and I was a Japanese American from the Chicago area, but till now, that difference had never surfaced as a tension in our friendship.

Recently, though, I had begun more and more to question my sense of my own identity. It had started by reading analyses of power and culture, such as those of Adorno, Foucault, Benjamin, and Berger. Books like Barthes's *Mythologies* and its analysis of colonialism and ideology hinted at a new way of looking at race, and this only increased in intensity as I stumbled on Fanon's *Black Skin, White Masks*. I read other black writers like Aime Cesaire, James Baldwin, Alice Walker. I went back and read the introduction and contents of *Aieeee!*, an anthology of Asian-American writing that a black fellow graduate student, Marilyn Waniek, had given to me, and which I'd never really looked at (after all, race was her concern). I'd started to see how much I had overidentified with white culture and the white canon, how much I had ignored and undervalued my own Japanese-American background and history. I'd begun to explore my feelings of alienation, self-hatred, and rage long hidden beneath my desire to be thought of as white.

And so Cathy and I were arguing about race. At one point, she complained that although I seemed to be publishing articles and poems concerning race, her poems on the subject weren't getting published. "I'd like there to be a dialogue," she said, "but it seems that my voice doesn't count." Later, I remarked to her that if I want to apply for a job, most often the person in charge of the hiring would be white. Whites rarely have the experience of applying for a job to a person of color. "Yeah, well, I know how that feels," she replied. "I'm a white middle-class woman and I can't get a teaching job anywhere."

At the same time she was making these remarks, my friend insisted on her good intentions, "I'm trying to deal with race as best as I can. I teach writers of color, I teach your works, I go hear writers of color read." She protested that she really didn't disagree with me about the basic issues, that she, too, wanted to live in a society without racism and was working to make this happen.

In my conversation with my friend, I did not point out to her that her focus on herself as an individual did not give an accurate picture of her or my reality. To her, the fact that I was being published and she was not meant that there was not a balanced dialogue in the literary world about the issues of race. Yet in reality, Cathy only had to turn on the news or open a paper to see her views about race affirmed. Even if she was not being published, writers who thought like her were, and still are, being published everywhere. To people of color, it's obvious that the views of whites dominate our cultural discourse about race, and that the people who control the media and other institutions of culture are white. Yet to my white friend, it seemed it was she as a white person who was being marginalized, not people of color.

Later, I talked to my wife, who is white, about this conversation. She and I had been having our own conversations about race and were about to reenter couples counseling to sort some things out. At times she seemed to understand the way I felt, and at times she worried she was agreeing with me simply to give in. But there was a trust there, a commitment and a sense of movement, I did not feel with my friend. (Later, a black friend would remark that the problem white women encountered in truly addressing racism was their loyalty to white men, particularly their husbands or lovers; this wasn't the case for my wife.)

My wife, at this point in time, was not quite willing to let go of her white friends over issues of race. She surmised that perhaps my friend was trying as best as she could.

"I, too, thought that initially," I replied, "that's why I didn't challenge her as much as I might have.

But later, I thought, No, it's not about trying. Cathy chose to believe certain things about the world, she chose to look at the world in a certain way, and she chose not to change. She chose to look at herself as the victim of racial politics. She chose not to examine what her resentment and envy might mean; she chose not to see the ways her views continued to support the racial status quo.

I can still recall vividly that walk with Cathy, her querulous tone, her confusion about why I had already broken off a friendship with another mutual white friend. She kept wanting to believe it was just differences in personalities, professional jealousies, perhaps. She wanted to believe that we did not really view things that differently, that we were on the same side. Yet even as she spoke, she seemed more and more distant from me. I felt she had been talking to herself or to someone else other than me, some vision of me she still clung to. Part of me sensed she'd reached a line and was not going to cross it. I had crossed, and there was no going back for me. She did not want to move, and she could not quite admit that.

And yet, in another sense, a gulf was revealed that had

always been there. Only I hadn't wanted to admit its existence. In a sense, I felt as if I had become a stranger, perhaps even to myself. The new part of me, or the long-buried part of me I'd claimed, remained beyond her view. Because if she truly saw it, she would have to change.

But perhaps my account makes all this clearer than it was, and I am granting myself a lucidity that comes only in retrospect. In my confusion I also felt guilty, as if I had done something wrong, as if I had somehow betrayed her or become suddenly this judgmental monster. My shifting sense of self scared me, as well as her. And, on a certain level, I was right to be scared.

After this, we had a couple of other subsequent conversations or arguments, but each ended in a kind of stalemate, a place not much different from our first argument. This sense of stasis led us both to feel it better to let the friendship go, without really formally marking an end. We just drifted apart, into other spheres. She never appears at the literary gatherings I go to now, mostly cabarets or spoken-word readings with a young multicultural, multiracial crowd. Nor do I attend the readings she attends, especially those of other white friends I've lost contact with.

In writing this, I cannot help but add that today my ex-friend has a teaching position in a local MFA program. I do not. There are many reasons for this difference, including my own reluctant relationship with teaching. Still, I believe that it is also true that the changes I have undergone in the ways I think about race and my own identity have had something to do with my job prospects in the town in which I live (and indeed elsewhere). I'm considered by many to be difficult and overly conscious of race, too up front with my views, and too angry. I've become the proverbial rageful man of color.

At the same time, I know I was not always this way. I had at one time many white friends. And virtually no friends of color.

A couple of years later, I'm standing outside on the sidewalk in January. It's Minneapolis and well below freezing. Snow whirls past, blown by an icy wind. I'm arguing with my black friend Alexs Pate, a writer. We're standing outside the house of a producer from the local public television station, with whom we've been discussing a film of the performance piece Alexs and I are creating. But right now the whole performance piece seems in jeopardy; the issues that have been brewing beneath the surface as we've worked together for a couple of months are now boiling over. Our voices are strained, not so much shouting, but exasperated, on edge.

Alexs is about my age, a poet and a fiction writer. He's someone I've known a few years as a member of the local literary scene, and in the last couple of years, I've become closer to. Alexs grew up in the black inner city of Philadelphia. I grew up in a white Jewish suburb. While I registered as a CO in college during the Vietnam War, he entered the navy. He has worked in a public relations firm and in corporate America, and only in recent years has he given himself over to his longtime desire to become a writer. His literary heroes are Langston Hughes, James Baldwin, Toni Morrison, John A. Williams, the first three whom I read only after I was drummed out of English graduate school and the last of which I have not yet read. His poetic background comes out of the Black Arts Movement and figures like Amiri Baraka and the Last Poets. My early literary heroes were Robert Lowell, John Berryman, Randall Jarrell, white Ivy League–educated males.

But it's not our literary forebears we're arguing about. It's our performance and our own individual working methods. Neither of us recalls exactly what sparked our argument. Perhaps it's trying to set a time for our next rehearsal or some pages of writing I've given Alexs or pages he hasn't written. But one topic leads to another, and it's all spilling out: Alexs is angry because he feels I'm always trying to control things. I'll decide to write on a topic before telling him, he says. Or I'll come to our meetings with ten pages written even before he feels we've had a chance to discuss things. When we come to a rehearsal space, it's me who arrives first and takes the best chair, the best music stand; then I stake out my area of the backstage and the stage even before he's there or has had a chance to settle down. The script has been put on my computer; I do revisions and do not always consult him first. The scripts are printed out in my usual typescript, one he finds much too small.

Part of me is puzzled at why Alexs is so angry. I'm always there on time, always waiting for him. Sometimes, after waiting so long, part of me wonders if he's going to show up at all. I write what I'm supposed to write and have to wait to see if he's going to write anything in response. It's me who's done all the paperwork for our grants, who has to badger him for things like his bio. As for taking the best chair or music stand, why would anyone notice or care? I just arrive before him and get ready. My stuff has to go somewhere; I have to sit somewhere on the stage. The script has to be on someone's computer, and why isn't he grateful about my doing the work to type and arrange his stuff?

Alexs's tone is louder, more angry than mine. Mine is exasperated, querulous. My argument isn't with what he's charging me with doing, just his interpretation of it. In other situations, it's me who's often the late one, so why get angry at something I expect others to forgive in me? At the same time, I try to tell myself I've seen him angrier, such as the time he blasted back at a white stage tech. I'm on safer ground than the white tech. Still, it's not like I'm black. Even though therapy has taught me the value of honest arguments, part of me is worried where this might lead. There's the risk that the whole project may blow apart, that he'll just decide the differences between us are just too difficult. Or even worse that those differences are due to something racist in me.

This is hardly the vision we started this piece with. For about a year we'd been talking about doing a performance piece together; then the Rodney King decision went down, the LA insurrection erupted, and all you saw on television were images of Korean store owners and local blacks in conflict, shooting at one another or one side defending their stores and the other looting them. The two of us believed that if we simply just sat on the stage, as friends, and conversed, that would be a revolutionary image. Where else would people see an African-American man and an Asian-American man working together?

So why were we fighting now? Was it personality? Was it race? What was going on between us?

Therapy and conversations with my wife had taught me it's best to get down to the basics of your fears and feelings. At a certain point, I threw up my hands and said to Alexs, "I just want to know that you care about me."

He looked at me, surprise in his face, and said, "Of course I care about you. I wouldn't be doing this show if I didn't. I wouldn't be out here in the cold talking with you like this."

Some part of me wanted to say, "But you don't show it."

But I knew it was enough to take him at his word. Still, I also felt scared. Compared to me, Alexs had a more forceful manner, was more willing to argue and engage in conflict. Like Rodney King, some voice inside me kept wanting to say, Can't we all just get along? But Rodney King's plea implied that we should simply stop talking about the difficult things that pulled us apart; it was a general message meant for a city. Alexs and I weren't a city of strangers, we were friends already. And part of me sensed we had now moved things to another level, that I should follow where our words had led us. Our mutual admissions of affection, though each in his own style, had changed the atmosphere between us. Perhaps I needed those admissions to be stated out loud in a way Alexs didn't.

Neither of us recalls exactly who took the next leap. I think Alexs said something about his feeling like my behaviors were those of a stereotypical Asian. I was like the theater version of the Asian nerd—always on time, always prepared, always doing more than anybody else. It made him feel uneasy. He just didn't work like that.

If a white friend had said something like this, this might have made me angry or at least have made me react more guardedly. But I placed Alexs's remarks in the context of his own battles with stereotypes. He hadn't said this as an insult. It was an admission, a revelation of what had been really going on inside him. At first, though, I didn't quite realize all these implications or how we were reaching a new level of honesty; I simply felt them. So I told Alexs I worked like that not to try to outdo him, but because that was simply my way of working.

"Yeah," he said, "but I don't work that way. I just think about things in my head."

I said I worried about getting things done on time. Then, for a second, we were both silent. Suddenly I realized something, something I probably would not have reached if Alexs hadn't admitted the way the stereotypes of Asians had entered into his thinking.

"Besides, I feel like I'm always behind."

"That's the way I feel," Alexs replied, referring to the amount of pages each of us had written.

"But I feel I'm always behind because I feel you know more about race than I do. I'm just catching up. I've been going around for years thinking that I was white. You've been dealing with this stuff and thinking about it a lot longer than I have. I feel like I've got to run as fast as I can to catch up and even if I do I'll never catch up."

We went on like this a while longer, through the conception of the piece, through the writing of the grants, the doling out of the script. Gradually it dawned on me: In certain ways, I told Alexs, each of us thought of the other in stereotypical terms—the nerdy Asian, the loafing black.

Just as importantly, each of us thought the other held more power and feared the other was taking control and leaving him behind. We both thought we were dealing from positions of weakness.

But now, each of us had come to see our differences were just that—differences. And they were actually what made us such a formidable team—if we could work together, if we could trust each other, if we could see the value in the way the other was working, if we could accept the other.

Neither of us had more power. Or: We both did.

And we both cared about each other, cared enough to stand

there out in the January Minneapolis snow and yell at each other and let our anger and resentment out and see where it led us. We'd both been willing to take that risk.

After that day, we argued from time to time, but the ground line had been established. We could even joke about these issues. They were part of our friendship, our working relationship. We both knew where the other stood.

Still, the basis of our friendship was more complicated than that. Certainly our coming together was. For I knew Alexs and I could never have become friends, could never have had this argument, had I not had arguments and broken off certain white friendships, had I not shown myself willing to let certain white friendships go down over my beliefs about race. He knew about my argument with Cathy about things like job prospects and race, and he knew that those arguments had been reenacted in various ways with other white friends, generally with the same results—the end of the friendship. If he hadn't seen me go through all that, if he hadn't seen I was willing to pay the price, he would never have trusted me enough to have that argument in the snow with me; he would never have been that open and vulnerable; he would never have believed I was someone who would "have his back."

II

During the late eighties, I found myself sitting on more and more multicultural panels and readings for audiences of color, and I was becoming friends with more artists of color. I began to see how what appeared to threaten white artists and audiences in my writing seemed to affirm and energize artists and audiences of color.

As I began to speak about white shame over the issue of race or how racism is based on a system of unequal distribution of power, I was sometimes faced with incomprehension or even anger on the part of white audience members. I would be speaking at, say, a small liberal arts college with three percent black students, one Filipino faculty member, and no black faculty, and people would tell me there was no racism in their town or campus. At the same time, blacks in the audience would come up afterward and embrace me or shake my hand, thank me for what I said, and speak somewhat bitterly of white denial. It seemed I was being presented with a choice about whom I would speak to, about where I was moving along the color line.

At a certain point, I wrote an article for *Mother Jones* on my breakup with a white male friend, a breakup that started with the *Miss Saigon* controversy. We had argued about the casting of a white actor in the role of a Eurasian and about the stereotypes in the plot of the musical. This led to more general arguments. One crucial sticking point was that he could not accept my insistence that I knew more about race than he did, that we didn't start there on equal ground.

This breakup was a landmark event for me. I knew my white friend loved me, I knew it pained him to end the relationship. But I felt that he would rather have given up the friendship than his beliefs about race, and these beliefs involved not just *Miss Saigon* but concerned the way he viewed his place and my place in the world.

As this breakup occurred, many of my white artist friends—

most were also his friends, too—were puzzled by it, and wanted to read it in light of personality or character differences. These friends were scared by my increasing anger about race and felt uneasy talking to me about the subject. And yet, unlike a couple of nonartist white friends, these artist friends seemed unable or unwilling to avoid the subject or let it go. I soon found myself in arguments with other mutual friends, like the argument with the white woman poet I described earlier. Gradually, I found myself spending less and less time with them.

## THE REMARK

It's often mere speculation or a casual off-the-cuff remark,
never quite a blatant stereotype, much less the direct
    inference,
god forbid, of inferior status: We're no longer in the
    dark ages.

So why bring it up? No one here at the table seems to
    have heard,
it's vanished in thin air, and should stay there, like some
    god madness,
a whispering that's only of my psyche, and not to be
    given in to,

some rage that set Othello upon Desdemona, Ajax on
    his cattle,
the streets of L.A. smoldering for days. Why risk all that?
And of course I need your friendship, need your approval,

perhaps even your love, such as it is, such as I sense now
it's become—a kind of bargaining, a silencing politeness
if not a smile. Better the old days I did not hear some

subliminal whispering, hidden in the words, sounding alarm.

Later, when my article about these very issues was published
in *Mother Jones*, many mutual friends were outraged at what they
took for a breach of privacy (though I didn't use any actual
names); they saw my article as an act of betrayal and a mean-
spirited attack. I received letters asking me if I'd become a racial
separatist or if I couldn't have white friends any longer. There was
speculation I was going to leave my wife. One friend wrote she
wasn't looking for a "guru" on race. Another quoted Wendell
Berry, who said the reward for destroying community was power.
(I pointed out that Berry was referring to huge corporate farm-
ing interests displacing family farms, and not one Japanese-
American writer arguing about race in a community of white
writers.) When my name came up as a suggested hire at a local
university, my article was used as an argument against me; so was
my appearance: "He dresses too well to be a minority." I found
myself eliminated from an editorial board I'd been on, and
somehow was never asked to write for the publication again.

I've written about all this before elsewhere, so I won't go
into much more of it here. Instead I want to recount here how
those events led to my friendship with Alexs.

A change in consciousness is hard to map with precision. I
can't recall exactly when I began to feel more comfortable with

a group of black artists than a group of white artists. But as many of my friendships with white friends began to unravel, I found that the person who could best explain my own process and feelings, who was the most supportive of my efforts to see myself as a person of color, who seemed to intuitively understand the anger and rage I was feeling, was Alexs Pate.

In a way, in my own naïveté and racism, I was somewhat shocked by this. Alexs was someone I was just becoming close to, yet he understood what I was going through during these breakups better than my wife, who was white, did. Moreover, his understanding of race was so far superior to mine or any of my white friends that I began to realize, with a certain feeling of shame, how I had underestimated him and his artistry.

Soon I realized that Alexs was in many ways much more qualified to help me through what I'd been experiencing than any white therapist I had been to.

I then realized that he was smarter than I thought he was.

And then it hit me: The reasons I hadn't seen this involved my own racism.

I realized if I held that much racism inside and I was another person of color, the strains of racism in our society went far deeper than I thought.

Obviously, Alexs and I could not have reached another level of intimacy if I hadn't gone through these realizations, if I hadn't come to terms with my own racism. Nor would he have trusted me enough to open himself to me and to try and help me.

Alexs told me that, in confronting racism, I needed to establish a base at which I thought my being and integrity was being threatened. There are conditions under which it's better to die than to continue living. But if you are not suffering these conditions, you need to negotiate your way through the difficulties that confront you; you need to rest; you need to know when it's time to fight and when to walk away.

He spoke of a black friend in the navy, who had been sprayed with a hose by a white petty officer. The friend lost his temper and smashed the officer in the head with a tool.

"I went to visit him in the brig," said Alexs, "and when I asked why he didn't think about the consequences, he said, 'That's something you can do, maybe it's because you have the abilities to do something with yourself. You see a future, but whatever the reason, it's something I can't do. I couldn't hold back.' That whole incident taught me something about survival."

Alexs recalled how an arts administrator had recently handed him a schedule for teaching as a writer in a high school. The administrator had constructed a schedule where Alexs was never in the classroom alone, there was always another white writer with him. All the other writers, who were white, had solo classroom appearances. Upon reading the schedule, Alexs chewed out the administrator and left the room, because if he had stayed in the room, there was no telling what he might have done.

The perception of the behavior of black men in this country is that they're constantly angry. Irrational. Indeed, I used to see Alexs, from a distance, as being an angry or bristly character. But as we became more intimate, I began to glimpse the enormous amount of anger and insults Alexs had to negotiate through his life, day by day; how difficult it had been for him to survive, to not explode in anger or implode in self-destruction. I realized with what grace and equanimity, with what quiet resolve, he went about his life. Alexs, his actions, made sense to me now; I saw a rationality and justification for aspects of his behavior that I didn't understand before.

At the same time, I saw that though I did not have the same amount of anger and had not suffered the same multitude of insults and slights, I was also fighting against a racist system. As I became conscious of the effect of this system, as I fought against it, it would be people like Alexs and writers like Baldwin or Malcolm X or Patricia Williams or bell hooks who could help me to survive. In seeing how necessary they were to my own survival, I was forced to examine how much of my life I had looked on African Americans as the Other: as a people to be pitied rather than to be admired. As victims but not as survivors and heroes and heroines; as the oppressed and not as leaders. As disadvantaged in comparison to whites or Asian Americans rather than as, in many instances, more perceptive and aware, with an understanding of America and its history that most whites and Asian Americans lack.

This is not to say I suddenly saw African Americans as saints; it is to say that I began to see how much I had been taught not to look at them as individuals, how little my experience or the culture had equipped me to understand their place and history in America, how little I knew of the ways black people think about themselves or whites. Instead, I was taught to dehumanize them, and this dehumanization had played itself out not only in my conceptualization of sexuality and race, but in my perception of artistic, intellectual, and spiritual matters as well. For instance, my reevaluation of Alexs's abilities and character paralleled a process I'd been undergoing in terms of aesthetic standards and the traditional canon; I'd come to understand how little of my literary training or my immersion in mainstream culture had prepared me to take an interest in the art of African Americans, much less to understand and evaluate that art or the lives and community it came out of. Similarly, I'd begun to understand more and more how our evaluations of morality in a historical context needed to be filtered through the lens of race. Figures like Malcolm X or the Black Panthers suddenly took on, in retrospect, a more complicated and human form in my mind, as well as a sense of how deeply I had been influenced by a white vision of what was right and what was wrong. This didn't mean that I agreed always with such figures, but it did mean I understood better the reasons for their words and actions.

Of course, such reevaluations were reinforced by the sense of outrage and remarks directed to me by whites as I made my own racial sojourn. My own sense of my role as a writer and a thinker had altered into something more oppositional, more at odds with the status quo, especially in regard to race. I felt a power and clarity in this, though of course still troubled by doubts. I saw myself aligned in a tradition that included figures like Baldwin, Baraka, and Aime Cesaire, and with a vision of the artist as an activist and builder of new traditions and institutions (I helped start locally an Asian-American arts organization, named the Asian American Renaissance, in part an allusion to the Harlem Renaissance). All this reinforced my belief in the power of art and the mutual sense of purpose I now shared with Alexs.

There are things Alexs and I share that have little or nothing to do with race—we're sports fanatics, for instance. We can go on elaborately about the benefits of the latest Timberwolves trade or their prospects for the upcoming playoffs. We'll talk about what's bothering us or intimate relationships in a way that's probably more open and fluent with feelings than most men (as I mentioned above, he's one of the most psychologically astute people I've seen). I'll talk to him about my dealings with my adolescent daughter; he'll talk to me about the breakup of a relationship or the start of a new one—each of us assuring and challenging the other, probing with questions only best friends can ask. If either of us gets down, the other is the first person we'll call.

We're roughly the same age and at the same stage in our careers: several books published, some national recognition but not as much as we think we merit. We can strategize about our writing or careers or criticize each other's work in a way someone older or younger could not. We both work in multiple genres—poetry, essays, drama, fiction. We're not scholars, and we lack the scholar's attention to details; our thinking tends to be both political and psychological, to be as concerned with society at large as with literature. We're both naturally night owls; as writers generally do, we cherish our solitude and solitary hours. We know we've worked hard to get where we are; we're probably both a little too unwilling to ask for anyone else's help, to seek a mentor. We want to do things ourselves, in our own way. We don't like to be beholden. If someone thinks that means we have chips on our shoulders, so be it.

But as I go through this litany of things that help bind us, it's hard to keep race out. Those chips on our shoulders—it's hard to separate them from the fact that we face a literary world where the gatekeepers are almost entirely white or from the fact that we often found ourselves in situations where there weren't any successful older writers of color to ask for help. Even with something like sports, race creeps in—from the perception of Randy Moss to the recent firing of Nolan Richardson. As I said to Alexs on the phone the other night: Indiana basketball coach Bobby Knight can beat up someone in Puerto Rico or head butt a player, but he was fired only when they caught him on tape choking one of his players. Arkansas coach Nolan Richardson did none of this; instead he was fired because he actually had the temerity to state an obvious truth—that as a black coach he was treated differently from a white coach.

I read such phenomena with a different lens than I used to, and this is in part due to what I've learned from Alexs. And I feel safe to express with Alexs an anger about such racial matters openly, and I know he feels the same with me.

Alexs says that one result of our friendship is that he began to realize that retiring some of his anger was better for him and for the people close to him. Part of the reason for this was that I developed anger; the development of my anger allowed him to give some of it to me or to let some of his go, because there were now two people fighting on the same issue. He could feel more comfortable and relaxed then; he could sit back and watch me fight for a while.

"And you're a much better fighter in some ways because you're coming from the left side. Like a southpaw. They're looking at me and you can cold cock 'em."

Conversely, when I am in Alexs's presence, I don't feel like the irrational angry Asian, too difficult to consider hiring for your faculty or inviting to your writers' conference. I'm simply myself, accepted for who I am. Safe, calm.

III

A few years ago, a Japanese American I know was teaching a multicultural literature course. When the course got to the writings of Asian Americans like Janice Mirikitani and Margaret Chin, many of the whites in the class became upset at the anger of the Asian-American authors. The Japanese-American teacher replied, "We've been reading people like Baraka and Nikki Giovanni and you weren't as upset by their anger." As the class continued to talk, the students revealed that they didn't expect Asian Americans to be angry; after all, they've been treated so well.

Whatever the individual quibbles my white friends have had with me or my writings, I don't see their reactions as simply personal or as solely a matter of personality or character. I see their reaction against a backdrop of the ways most whites look at their friendships with individuals of color, particularly Asian Americans, and the ways they view a racial issue. For many years, I lived an unconscious life that constantly tried to repress anything in my experience that related to race; the friends I had then were comfortable with that repression. When I started to break down that repression, I had to look not only at my identity but also at *their* identity, at the ways they were comfortable with that repression and what that told me about the way they saw me, about what they meant when they said they loved me. (After all, Scarlett loved Mammy and where did that get Mammy?)

With other whites with whom I am still friends, I now recognize a zone of intimacy I do not cross, certain feelings I choose not to talk about. I know I avoid bringing up my racial anger in ways that I would naturally do with friends of color. Nor do I feel—in the way I do with most friends of color—that if some particularly ugly or difficult issue or incident came up, I could count on these white friends to back me up. I can't help but sometimes feel that they believe race is simply my problem and not theirs.

Along with friends, there are other things I've had to give up. Among them is the Asian-American dream of being the "model minority." Like many other Asian Americans, I believed that if I worked hard and produced work with quality, all would be fine, I would be accepted as an equal (I am constantly chagrined with how, on an emotional level, something inside me still wants to believe this). But my experiences with arts organizations, judging panels, writing programs, and universities— most English departments look no different from the front office of former Cincinnati Reds owner Marge Schott—as well as the experiences of other friends and artists of color, have shown me this is not so.

Still, my wife and Alexs have told me that what I have yet to do is write about what I loved in the friends I have lost; is describe what I miss from those circles or art or pleasures I no longer feel can engage me, what has hurt so much in this transition I am still making. But it feels too difficult and bewildering to do this; some part of me doesn't see the point of it. It's much easier for me to be angry at those who have disagreed with the choices I have made, who were so frightened by my growing identification with other people of color. It's easier for me to analyze the structures of white cultural domination or to speak in more general terms of who Asian Americans are and where we might go. It's easier to speak of challenging the tradition and its critical standards or to concoct strategies to "diversify" and "empower."

I think about the white friends I have lost often, though not so constantly as before. They appear to me in dreams as awkward, sometimes invasive, presences. I see them in life and we smile politely. I still want their approval, want their love. The ache of distance does not go away.

The other day, I saw a former white friend in a local bookstore and smiled hello. He came up and shook my hand. It was an awkward yet open gesture, which I did not know how to take. We said nothing more. He was having lunch with another former friend. I did not sense any acrimony in him, though I felt some, along with a renewed sense of pain. Though I had no concrete proof of this, I felt that what had happened between us had had many more repercussions for me than for him.

Could I describe these former friends, their humor and intelligence, their skills as writers, the various ways they've contributed to the local writing community? Could I write about them in such a way that you would see them as good, caring people? Could I describe the ways they have chosen to live their lives and create a three-dimensional portrait, as if out of a novel? I don't know. There is a great bitterness in me. And anger. Jealousy perhaps—of their continued sense of community and the advantages, professional and personal, that community provides them. None of this means they aren't good, caring people who have given to others. Part of me feels that the reason they are no longer in my life is a mystery, a bad dream. And part of me knows this severance was necessary. That I have still more difficult choices ahead.

As for Alexs and me, we continue to work and perform together. We call each other up late at night and talk, go out for dinners at a local Italian restaurant where we hash over reviews of our books, our individual writing projects, criticize each other's work, and plan new coproductions. Occasionally we go to a Timberwolves game or go golfing together, an image that amuses our mutual friends: two middle-aged men of color, one Asian with ponytail, one black with dreads, playing what Alexs and I have called the white man's game (but of course this was before Tiger, that Afro-Asian-American superstar).

Both of us spend time meeting and mentoring young writers of color, attending a spoken-word scene where Asian Americans and African Americans mix together, perform together, and sit in audiences together in ways that never occurred when we were younger. Back in the day—which isn't that long ago—we were among only a handful of local artists of color and our audiences were mostly white. Now I'll get up on stage with a half-dozen younger Asian-American writers who are as open or even more so in their anger over race or their explorations of such topics as race and sexuality. I'm no longer the lone Asian who has crossed the line and gone crazy. A few weeks ago, in a tribute series arranged by younger writers of color, I was honored by both local black and Asian-American writers for my work in the community as well as my writing and teaching. Alexs spoke there about some of the trials I've gone through and tried to set a historical context for the younger writers; I felt both protected and loved.

I never see my old white writer friends at these events I go to; their scene is older, still as white, and more suburban than urban. What all this means for the state of race in America, I don't know. Alexs always tells me our time is coming, our audience is coming. I try to believe him. He bolsters me now more as his career has taken off, shooting somewhat beyond mine, and I'm pleased to find that I have few feelings of jealousy, that I see his successes as part of our common cause, that we are determined to pull each other along; what benefits one will somehow help the other. We're older now, calmer, perhaps more focused on our own particular work. We don't do hip-hop or rap or even participate regularly in the spoken-word scene. We're the elders, though Alexs sometimes bridles and wants to shun this role ("I refuse to be put out to pasture like that").

Still, he's the one who carries reading glasses that I borrow to read the menu in the dimly lit upscale restaurant where we usually meet. When I hand his glasses back, he chides me about my vanity: "You ought to get your own glasses." I tell him at least I'm honest to people about my age. He laughs and tells me his age is no one else's damn business. Then I ask him what he's going to order. More often than not, we share an appetizer, usually calamari. When the waiter comes up, I know Alexs is going to explain he's lactose intolerant, he wants this pasta or other dish but without cheese. Alexs knows I'm going to order some big hunk of meat, and that later, when we're handed the dessert menus, I'll ask for his reading glasses once again.

# THE VALUE OF THINGS NOT SAID: SOME THOUGHTS ON INTERRACIAL FRIENDSHIP

## Maurice Berger

*This Republic has, indeed, told itself and Black
people nothing but lies, which is the very definition
of the betrayal of the social contract.*

—JAMES BALDWIN,
*The Evidence of Things Not Seen*

It was at a typical art world event fifteen years ago, an opening reception for an exhibition at a New York art gallery, that I first meet my friend Shirley Verrett. I knew that Shirley was the wife of the painter Louis LoMonaco, one of the artists in the show, and I anticipated that she might be there. As soon as I noticed her—and it was not hard to notice Shirley at that moment, a statuesque black woman wearing a turban and radiant blue evening dress in a somber crowd of artists and critics dressed mostly in black—I knew I wanted to talk to her. I got up the nerve to introduce myself, but as I extended my hand and uttered my name, my voice broke. I could not disguise the fact that I was awestruck, for I was meeting not just a famous diva, but one of my mother's favorite opera singers.

"Miss Verrett, may I tell you a story about my mother?" I continued, my voice quivering. "I have waited almost ten years to tell you this."

Shirley nodded yes.

The story I would tell concerned the last time my mother saw Shirley Verrett perform. In the 1940s and early 1950s, my mother had been a promising young opera singer. My father married her in 1954 on the condition that she give up music to be the keeper of his house and the mother of his children. Years of bitterness about her lost career gradually evolved into a bittersweet admiration for those women who had made it. My mother lived vicariously through them. She could not afford an opera ticket, but opera biographies borrowed from the library, a careful eye to newspaper reviews and gossip columns, and the constant monitoring of a few favorite singers who appeared regularly on television served as her connection to the opera world.

Shirley Verrett was one of her "girls," a mezzo-soprano whose dazzling performances at the Metropolitan Opera, Covent Garden, and La Scala made her a media darling. In the spring of 1978, a month before she died of breast cancer, my mother watched Verrett perform on the PBS series *Live from*

*Lincoln Center*. She had recently read that the singer, after years of singing mezzo parts, had expanded her repertoire to include soprano roles. My mother, who was a soprano and who appreciated Verrett more as a performer and media personality than for her mezzo roles, saw this performance as a chance to size up her vocal range. Emaciated and stooped over in her wheelchair, my mother sat silent and motionless as Verrett sang. Tears slowly rolled down her face as she listened to the diva's moving finale—Mozart's *Exultate Jubilate*—a favorite recital piece from my mother's student days. It was the last time I would see joy on my mother's face.

As soon as the last words left my mouth, Shirley reached out to me. There we stood, tearfully hugging each other, oblivious to both the art and the artists around us. We exchanged phone numbers, but I assumed I would never hear from her again. The story I told must have moved Shirley greatly, however, because several months later, out of the blue, she invited me to dinner. We soon began seeing each other socially. Phone conversations and dinner dates progressed to weeklong stays at the summer home that Shirley and Lou shared in upstate New York. I began accompanying Shirley to some of her concerts and operas, sitting backstage in her dressing room as she prepared for her performances.

In the beginning, our friendship was reverential and polite, the result of a mutual idealization—I was enthralled by Shirley's talent and glamour; she, as it turned out, by the essays and books of mine that she had begun to read—that gave us little room to let our hair down. Eventually, infatuation evolved into deeper and more realistic feelings and expectations, which in turn progressed to trust. The strength of this trust has allowed us to challenge each other in ways that would not earlier have been possible. We have pushed each other in matters of career, health, and family. We have shared secrets. We have argued. We have been there in difficult times, often in midnight phone conversations after our partners have gone to bed.

The trust that supports our friendship would not be possible without honesty. If there is one thing that Shirley and I have in common, it is our mutual hatred of indirectness and deceit. We have discussed many things—few subjects have been untouchable, in fact—but no issue, perhaps, has been as consequential as race. We have talked about things that white and black people rarely discuss with each other: Shirley's rage at the white folks who kept her in her place in the South of the 1930s and 1940s; my own adolescent flirtation as a white person with racial prejudice; interracial relationships and marriage (Lou is Italian American); the issue of racism itself. The experience of this and other relationships has taught me that frankness about race can be an important and enriching part of interracial friendship.

In light of the problematic, divided state of contemporary race relations, such candor is hard to achieve. The social and cultural inroads of the 1960s and 1970s toward integration have all but evaporated, resulting in the increasing resegregation of America's racial landscape. More than half a century after the birth of the modern civil rights movement, we remain a nation of racial isolationists—people and communities alienated from one another, and locked into attitudes, behaviors, and lies driven by primitive emotions and phobias. We erect emotional and physical walls that shield and isolate us from each other. We rarely talk across racial lines. We rarely acknowledge the underlying uncertainties and anxieties that make interracial relation-ships uncomfortable and unlikely.

The alienation of the races, and the concomitant fear of interracial intimacy, is deeply rooted in the Western psyche. In the nineteenth and well into the twentieth century, many sci-entists and cultural theorists viewed contact between the races as innately unhealthy. These arguments, of course, were moti-vated not by concern for the well-being of black people but rather by anxieties about the corruption of the white race and the downfall of civilization that would be its result. In the con-text of such thinking, interracial friendship was viewed as unwholesome, interracial sex or marriage as abnormal or pathological, and the children of those unions as inexorably feeble and impaired. At the turn of the last century, the novel-ist Abel Hermant wrote of the inevitable failure of romantic love between the races:

> *Differences of race are irreducible and between two beings who love each other they cannot fail to produce exceptional and instructive reactions. In the first superfi-cial ebullition of love, indeed, nothing notable may be manifested, but in a fairly short time the two . . . in striv-ing to approach each other strike against an invisible par-tition that separates them. Their sensibilities are divergent; everything in each shocks the other; even their anatomical conformation, even the language of their ges-tures; all is foreign.*

If Hermant's observations were motivated by the lies of white supremacy, his description of the foreignness and discomfort of racial interaction was not without a grain of truth. The black psychiatrist and revolutionary Franz Fanon spoke of a similar, albeit more violent, reaction whenever he encountered the smug, rapierlike gaze of the white colonialist in Africa of the 1950s: "I met the white man's eyes," he wrote, "as if in an anticipation of an amputation, an excision, a hemorrhage that spattered my whole body with black blood." The allergic interface between black and white bodies described by both authors—one observed through the racist logic of pseudo-science, the other through the lens of oppression—in more subtle ways continues to charge and define interracial contact. The discomfort educed by interracial intimacy impels most of us to avoid such contact, suppress or deny the feelings it elicits, or sublimate these feelings into unconscious, often repellent behavior. Tactics of avoidance have become commonplace across racial lines in everyday interaction—the awkward movements and nervous tics, the averted eyes, the crossed arms, the evasive or hostile gestures that often overtake the body when a person of a different color comes into view.

This evasiveness, no doubt discomforting to white people, can be devastating to black people who must live with the daily effects of hurtful, albeit subtle, forms of racism. Many times, I have heard such stories from my black friends. One of the first anecdotes Shirley told me about her experiences with racism concerned the insulting behavior of a celebrated American conductor during rehearsals for a concert version of an opera in Europe in the early 1970s. The conductor stopped her singing to say that she—unlike the white, European musicians who performed alongside her—was interpreting her arias incorrectly, adding grace notes and other flourishes where they did not belong. Shirley, a rigorously trained opera singer who is renowned for the skill and depth of her musical interpretation, reminded the conductor that such grace notes were indeed correct. He scoffed at this suggestion and turned to the white singers, instructing them to "show Miss Verrett the right way" to sing the music. Shirley, both angry and hurt, refused to listen. She was soon vindicated: a number of European music critics— among opera's harshest and most demanding evaluators—went out of their way to congratulate Shirley for being the only singer in the production to interpret the music correctly.

Black people continually experience this kind of prejudice— words and actions that are often far more indirect or unconscious, and thus they are usually heard and felt between the lines of communication. Such racism, of course, takes many forms: the patronizing comment of the white friend who insists that you are only imagining a racist incident or slight; the disturbing avoidance of the sales clerk who refuses to place change directly in the palm of your hand, or the cabdriver who will not stop for you; the unnerving surveillance of the security guard or policeman who has profiled you as a thief; the insulting remark of the merchant or the bank officer who automatically assumes that your credit is no good; the condescending behavior of the teacher who takes for granted your ignorance.

James Baldwin wrote in *The Evidence of Things Not Seen* that the observant and circumspect writer, in search of the true meaning of what he is being told, never takes what he hears at first value. He listens "to what is *not* being said," wrote Baldwin, "to what he's *not* being told." The author's point, made in the context of a polemic against racism in America, is also a metaphor for black people who, as a matter of survival or safety, must always listen to what is not being said. This information is important, for to ignore the prejudice that lies just below the surface of interracial contact is to disregard the hidden agendas that are designed to perpetuate white power and to keep black people in their place.

Despite its promise of undying loyalty and trust, intimate friendship is not immune to these agendas. Relationships of friendship and love are fraught with fear and vulnerability. They can incite feelings of envy, jealousy, competitiveness, rejection, and hurt. They can feel unequal, onesided, or unsupported as the interpersonal dynamics of power and control shift. They can motivate bad behavior and acting out. Intimacy between the races is innately more difficult, given the societal and cultural proscriptions and anxieties around racial difference and interracial contact. Thus, the hypervigilance necessary for surviving racism in the society at large—a watchfulness that does little to engender the mutual trust necessary for friendship—can easily work its way into interracial relationships.

More than anything, it is honesty that can help break down these barriers to intimacy. In bringing out into the open the unspoken anxieties, discomfort, and prejudices that we normally sublimate into reflexive conduct or actions, we are doing more than just being candid about our feelings. We are making these feelings available for discussion, self-analysis, and understanding. Of course, friendship must build toward such uncompromising honesty. Without deeper intimacy and trust, it may well be easier to sustain friendship by *not* saying what is on our minds or revealing the secrets of our bigotry. But eventually, candor can enrich and empower interracial intimacy. It is important for black people and even more so for white people, who all too often underplay, misunderstand, or simply cannot see the extent to which their own evasive or inscrutable conduct mirrors the racism that is experienced every day by their black peers. While the sharing of painful or even hurtful secrets and emotions may be difficult, even in close friendships, frankness about race, especially about one's own racial attitudes and perceptions, is preferable to the avoidance and acting out that keeps the other person guessing and off-guard.

In thinking of the power of honesty in interracial friendship, I am reminded of an instance in my relationship with Shirley where a lie of omission seemed preferable to the truth. In our first encounter and for many years thereafter, I did not tell her the whole story about my mother's adoration of her. I could not tell Shirley that she was one of the few black people to win my mother's approval. For more than twenty years, my family lived in a predominantly black and Hispanic housing project on the Lower East Side of Manhattan. Despite her surroundings, my mother hated black people. She called them *schwartzes*. She saw justification in their deaths. (Dr. King "deserved to die," she once told me, because he was a "troublemaker.") She believed that she was smarter, classier, and prettier than her black neighbors. More than anything, my mother resented her proximity to blackness: She hated living in the projects. She hated the dark, Sephardic skin she worked so hard each morning to conceal under layers of white makeup. It took me five years to build up the courage to let Shirley know that my mother had chosen to overlook the color of her skin, a blackness that normally would have rendered her less than human in my mother's eyes. To my mother, Shirley Verrett possessed a talent that was undeniable. She was an exceptional "*schwartze*"—so beautiful, soft-spoken, and elegant—who despite her rich mahogany skin was "practically white."

This story neither surprised nor upset my friend. "I am relieved you told me this," was all Shirley would say. I, too, was relieved, for protecting the secret of my mother's racism always felt dishonest. It was a secret I always felt obligated to conceal from my friends, black and white, lest I offend them, or more to the point, lest they think less of me. But in keeping this secret, I was rendering invisible an important part of myself—the part of me that adored my mother but hated her thinking about race, the part of me that once believed she was right, the part of me that loved my father for rejecting her bigotry, the part of me that has struggled to be more like him.

This is not to say that Shirley was unaware of my racial politics. We had talked about race before. She had read my work on the subject. But knowing a person's ideas about racism is not the same as knowing a person's prejudices. Shirley was one of the first friends with whom I shared the story of my mother's bigotry. Perhaps it was the coincidence of my mother's warped adulation of her that compelled me to tell her my secret. By revealing the truth about my mother, I was starting the process of revealing to my friend where my heart and soul—and not just my head—lay on the question of race. With this honesty, I was telling Shirley a number of things: that my allegiance to whiteness was not so tribal and absolute that I could not see and understand white racism; that I was willing to confront my own racism and that of my family; that I trusted and respected my friend enough to tell her the truth.

As it turned out, this early demonstration of candor—which was soon followed by Shirley's own frankness about race—was a turning point in our friendship. While we both needed a degree of intimacy to build up enough trust to be truthful with each other, the honesty that emerged from this trust ultimately helped us break through the emotional barriers that make interpersonal interaction between white and black Americans difficult. It opened the door to discussions about race as well as many other important and challenging issues. In the end, honesty has become a form of generosity and grace in our relationship, a gift that has spared us both from the wearisome practice of listening for the words not said, the things not told.

# GRINGO
# RESERVATIONS

## Sandra Guzmán

I was ten years old the first time I was called a spic. A gringa, or Americana, as we called white girls, hurled the insult. Her name was Kathy, and she was one of the white girls who lived across the street from me in the neighborhood where I grew up. My friends and I were playing handball, and Kathy was upset that our ball had dared to venture into her yard. She threw it back but not before warning me not to let that dirty spic ball fall into her garden again. Aixa, Chubby, and John John, my scraggly group of childhood playmates, urged me to jump that "white trash" for insulting me. But I didn't. I caught the ball and went back to the game. I didn't know what Kathy meant. Up to then, spic had not been part of my vocabulary. I had been in this country only a year, and my English was still rudimentary. Later, sitting on my fourth-floor tenement fire escape—my garden—overlooking the cement street, I asked John John what the big deal was with the word "spic." Having been called a dirty Puerto Rican spic many, many times (even though his parents are Ecuadorian), he explained its implications. Since then, no one has gotten away with calling me a spic without my physically or verbally defending myself. The incident left an indelible mark on my life, and set the tone for the way I came to view white folks.

John John, Chubby, and Aixa—my neighborhood buddies—were all Latinos. I suppose I could have befriended the other three girls on my block—before the spic incident, that is—but Kathy, Patty, and Doreen were Americans—and therefore off limits to me. The Americana girls lived across the street with all the other white people. They were Irish American, Polish American, Italian American and German American. They lived in the one- and two-family homes; we, the black and brown folks, lived in the tenements. They had the sunny side of the sidewalk; we had the shaded part. In the summer, we had the advantage because it was cooler on our side. It was a typical immigrant working-class city neighborhood in northern Jersey—a melting pot fantasy, it was not.

The racial dynamics of my New Jersey block had a Cold War atmosphere: The gringas and gringos never crossed the street to our side of the sidewalk, and we never crossed to theirs. As long as each respected the invisible border—determined by race, class, language barriers, and stereotypes—all was cool on the block. Even though my mother never explicitly handed down an edict prohibiting me from playing with the gringas, I knew it was something I should not even try. When it came to these girls, I sensed treacherous waters. As the granddaughter of a fisherman, I knew, even then, that only a fool challenges the sea.

I had very little in common with the Americanas. They

were my age but acted much older. Kathy was petite and chubby and wore her shorts so high that her butt cheeks peeked out. Patty started bleaching her hair blond at eleven and spiked and teased it high above her head. I am convinced that she was the first to sport what is today popularly known as "New Jersey hair." Doreen, the youngest of the three, wore so much blue eye shadow and blue eyeliner that they nearly overpowered her sky blue eyes. They studied in Catholic schools; we went to the local public schools. They dressed like young strippers and wore high heels to play tag and other kid games. They cursed like sailors—even to their moms and dads. But all three girls were very popular with the boys on our very boy-heavy block.

Even though I don't remember my mom ever saying anything bigoted about las Americanas, I do recall that she felt they were too *liberadas*—independent. In her eyes, they were guilty of two cardinal sins: They did not respect elders; and they were not virgins, as Latina girls were expected to be, even if they seldom were. And Mom certainly did not want me or her other daughters, good Puerto Rican *hijas*, to be "contaminated" by any of those gringo ways—talking back and disrespecting elders, having premarital sex, not honoring *la familia*, and oh lord, sporting the over-the-top butt-'n'-boob revealing fashions.

It was a different case altogether in the streets. Whenever white people were talked about, it was always with an air of *sospecha*—suspicion. I'd hear that gringas were loose, easy lays and *sucias*; in other words, trash. Gringos—the males—were cold and untrustworthy. All the *viejitos* and *viejitas*, the elders who were so revered on my block, were openly vocal in their distrust of the white folks—white children included. I think they feared what they thought would become of us, the good Latina girls, if we befriended the Americanas. American girls, they'd say, had different *costumbres*, habits, which were unbecoming to young Latinas. We had responsibilities in the home, from helping with the cooking and other household chores to baby-sitting our younger siblings. In addition, we were expected to leave home in a white wedding gown with a husband in hand, and not with a roommate or a live-in *novio*, something that was not unusual for the older Americanas.

Even though we lived on a one-way street, our mistrust was a two-lane highway. The white folks across the street were just as wary about us, the Latin and black families who lived in the dilapidated buildings facing their homes. I remember the guarded looks hurled at us. There was always an air of disgust and arrogance whenever they glanced our way.

One summer, during a scorching heat wave, the oldest teenager in the group, Luis, took to opening a hydrant that was located on their side of the sidewalk. The torrential stream stripped the sticky, muggy, Jersey-brick summer heat off our little bodies. That pump became our backyard swimming pool, our South Hampton beach, our Martha's Vineyard getaway. It also became an instant car wash to all the cars that passed. But every time Luis opened the pump—an illegal act—the white ladies, mothers to Kathy, Doreen, and Patty, would call the cops on us. One time, the ladies pointed out Luis's building to the cops, who then arrested Luis. I can still feel the anger that raged inside me that day when the pump was turned off and

Luis was hauled off to jail. Hair wet, clothes soggy, and tears streaming down my little face, I breathed gringo hatred. I breathed it in deep.

These racist experiences planted doubts about white people in my developing soul, yet I held on to hope, still wishing to meet white people as nice as the ones that I saw on my favorite television shows: *The Brady Bunch*, *Laverne and Shirley*, and *Happy Days*. Years went by, and I never met those nice white people on the block or in school. I thought for sure I'd find them in college.

My first semester, I was placed in a triple dorm room with two other females, both white. I arrived at the room that first day and found that my roommates had left me with the top bunk, which had the thinnest mattress. There was no talk about rotating the beds as others in triple rooms had agreed. It felt wrong and unfair, but I didn't want to whine. "I'm a big girl now," I remember thinking, and "This is the first day of school, no time to complain." In a weird way, I think I didn't press the issue because I was going to school on loans and financial aid scholarships while my roommates were paying full tuition. Maybe deep inside, my feelings of inferiority kept me from standing up and making a perfectly fair request. Besides, I also didn't want to deal with the implications if they said no. So, from the first day, I sensed that class, culture, and race had already created thick walls between us. The sad truth was that none of us attempted to break those barriers down. After all, we had very little in common: They were suburban and in the upper tax bracket, and I was from a working-class Jersey ghetto. This was way before hip-hop or Eminem made the hood a "cool" place to call home.

On spring and holiday breaks, my roommates traveled to Paris, Milan, Florida; I took a train to my Jersey hood. It seemed like I was the only Latina in a dormitory that housed close to four hundred students. If there were more Latinos, they were paper Latinos, unwilling to identify *con la raza*. I had never felt so alone.

On two occasions, one of my roommates invited me to her palatial home. It was an afterthought—she was planning the trip with our other roommate, and then suddenly realized that I was in the room, too. During the first visit, a relative asked me if people who lived in Puerto Rico still walked around in grass skirts like they did in Hawaii. How does one respond? I played stupid and actually explained, carefully and thoughtfully, the contemporary nature of Puerto Rican society. I thought, "Hey—this is just benign gringo ignorance." Then I went on a second visit, still thinking these folks were not that bad, that they were just country bumpkins, and I, the city slicker Rican, would show them another kind of Boricua. On this the second and final visit, yet another relative told me her favorite movie was *West Side Story*. Is that really how it happens in your part of town? she asked. How does one respond? I was not sure if I should laugh or take offense. I smiled tightly and somehow summoned the words to explain to this woman fact from fiction. I remember feeling naked and vulnerable, but knowing at the same time that I had to stand up for *mi gente* and for me.

My white roommates were thoughtful with each other and cordial to me. For instance, they waited for each other in the mornings to go to breakfast together. If I happened to be ready when they were, they would walk hurriedly past me and say, You coming? They never waited for an answer. But I cherished those mornings in the empty dorm room. Yes, I poked around in their stuff and flopped on their good beds. Then I turned on the radio and danced alone to Hector Lavoe, Ismael Rivera, Frankie Ruiz, Run DMC, and others.

My white roommates, who became close friends, had intimate conversations that always seemed to stop when I entered the room. They never made outwardly cruel, much less racist, jokes or comments about blacks or Latinos in front of me. But there were lots of assumptions—like, "Wow, *you* aced that history test?" There was a consistent presumption of racial, cultural, and intellectual superiority on their part—they seemed genuinely surprised that I could be as competent and smart as they. I found myself thinking back to my block—at least the white folks in my hood let me know how they felt. With these Americanas, my gringa roommates, the isms were subtle, nuanced. We had pretend relationships—the kind where you make believe all is good on the surface, but underneath you know it's a farce. You are guarded, always holding back, your heart and soul remaining closed to any potential relationship that might otherwise blossom. Our conversations consisted of the morning and evening hellos and good nights. I remember wishing, for just a second, to be white like them so that I would be able to be part of their white-girl club. It was not so much that I found their clique so attractive; I simply hated always being the other.

I regret that I never directly addressed the negative assumptions that my roommates made about me, the other roommate. I pretended to be oblivious. People of color often pretend that the assumptions white people make do not sting; we ignore them or feign invincibility. It is our way of pushing the pain away and moving forward: It is our way of surviving. But the wounds of these assumptions and obvious slights fester and hurt. My roommates never talked about the obvious—the cultural, racial, and class gulf that existed between us. I am sorry that we didn't. It would have been a chance for each of us to grow.

Sophomore year I was able to choose roommates, and I went with the familiar and supportive—women who looked like me and who shared my class background and struggles. There was a fellow Latina by way of the Dominican Republic, a black woman from South Jersey, a U.S.-born-and-raised Filipina. In each of these friendships, I found no need to explain my essence, to fight to be heard, or to leave intimacy at the welcome door mat. I did not have to hide, to watch myself. These women did not question my talent, intelligence, and capacity to achieve. Our exchanges were soulful and genuine. Even though we have gone our separate ways, I remember those friendships with warmth and know that they played a very important role in my life journey. In my intimate circle of friends today, there are no gringos or gringas.

I wish I could tell you that it is only a coincidence that I have no cherished white amigas or amigos, but that would make me a hypocrite—I would say it only to save public face and, even worse, deceive myself. Race *has* been a major factor in why I have no close white friends. To put it bluntly, I don't trust white people, and without trust, there can be no real friendship. Early on, Mami hammered into my head her belief that only my four siblings could be my friends. With others—non-blood relatives, that is—she said I could have *hasta la puerta* friendships—friends up to the doorstep. You can play all you want outside, she'd say to me as a child, but those schoolyard or neighborhood buddies aren't really your friends. They were doorstep buddies—superficial friends to be left in the yard. The doorstep for Mom was a metaphor for the heart. Friendships *hasta la puerta*—that is probably the best way to describe my relationships with Americanas and Americanos today.

One should not have to walk on eggshells among friends, I think. One should not have to translate one's essence, either. With black and brown folk—people whose story I know because it is always, on some level, my own—I have nothing to explain. With white people, I have had to field questions like, Are those green bananas or yellow bananas your people fry? Did you know Ricky Martin before America discovered him? Sometimes there are compliments; my favorite is, You speak English so well! Even to the learned and well-meaning Americanos and Americanas that have entered and exited my life, I have always had to translate parts of myself, despite our common command of the Queen's English.

This has been a painful essay to compose—both in the quiet privacy of my heart and here, in this public space. I have agonized over my admissions because I know they have the potential to paint me as a racist, something I confidently know I am not. But in these tough times of racial and religious intolerance, we need to try something new in America's racial discourse: audacious candor, both with each other and with ourselves. If more of us reflected honestly about our individual biases and talked about them, we could get closer to moving beyond this hellish legacy of racism.

I am a descendant of slaves; I am a survivor of colonization. In my private and most vulnerable spaces, I will protect myself from those who have hurt me. Is it fair to label all white people the same? To ask the descendants of colonizers and slaveholders to pay for atrocities they played no part in? To hold strangers accountable for the racist childhood and teenage experiences I endured? Absolutely not. Truth is, deep down, I am open. I am, like the great philosopher Cornel West, a prisoner of hope in matters of race. My heart is not closed to having a gringo friend. However, as my mother would say, these friendships will happen only under certain conditions. I must be met halfway. I am willing to acknowledge my biases and help destroy them. My potential gringo or gringa friends must be willing to recognize theirs, as well. They will have to drop the superiority complex, recognize me as an equal, understand how white privilege and power have wreaked havoc in the world generally, and have given them a skewed sense of reality, specifically. This Americana or Americano will have to be willing to challenge myths, tear down walls, and then, side by side with me, build sturdy, honest bonds. The kind of gringo friend that I am open to has to be willing to see the world as I see it, with Afro- and Latinogenic eyes. Until then, I am perfectly happy that my inner circle is a tight rainbow of glorious blacks, beiges, and browns.

# ON THE
# POSSIBILITY-FILLED
# EDGE OF THE CONTINENT

## Pam Houston

This summer while teaching in Provincetown, Massachusetts, I met a black woman named Abigail and we began a friendship that—in spite of the three thousand miles that separate us for most of the year—I expect to grow and thrive.

Provincetown is, in my opinion, the most wonderful place in America. It is a place where, from the minute you arrive, you feel that anything on earth might happen to you. A place where you can be anything you want to be, where the line between all that is the self and all that is the other can get willingly and happily blurred. Perhaps it is the contrast between the tight-lipped clapboard houses and the cars full of cross-dressed debutantes that cruise Commercial Street; between the stately branch office of the Seaman's Bank and the sex toy store that sits catty-corner from it; between the sound of the horn on the Land's End lighthouse and the techno beat at the daily pick-up scene known as the four o'clock tea dance. Or perhaps it has something to do with being on the very tip of the continent, the way Cape Cod rolls out its arm, and makes first a muscle, and then a fist, inviting you to the very edge, to step through whatever door or window you've been imagining.

When I am in Provincetown I am my best self, my least self-critical self, my most authentic self. I think it is the town's eclectic population and playful spirit that leads me to ask myself questions that I don't ask during other weeks of the year. Such as, Am I really a bisexual? Do I secretly wish to be a cross dresser? Am I, in fact, a gay man? Am I actually a black woman? I might go so far as to say that if one doesn't ask herself such questions in Provincetown, one isn't paying much attention to all that is in the air.

I should probably clarify at this point that I am a white woman, married—faithfully, and knock-on-wood, happily—to a white man, and yet I am also a person who falls in love almost constantly, with a new friend of either sex, with a bowl of chilled beet soup, with the way the late August light plays across the dunes of Race Point on the back of the fist of Cape Cod. I may use the expression "falling in love" broadly here, but not lightly. To be in love for me is to be alive. I only have to look up from my computer to see dozens of things I am in love with: my young Irish wolfhound, Mary Ellen; my new grape-colored KitchenAid mixer; a piece of fabric I brought back from Bali on its dragon-headed rung. Outside the window is my Paso Fino gelding, Deseo, who came in from the pasture with a nose full of porcupine quills yesterday and had to be sedated, and beyond him the aspen groves in their full September yellows, saffrons, and tangerines.

In Provincetown, Abigail spoke bravely and articulately about all the things that matter. She treated herself and others with humor and compassion. She wore a brown and black cotton shirt that rippled in the wind and showed off her strong, lovely shoulders. That I was there, on the possibility-filled edge of the continent, was at least one reason that I got brave enough to think Abigail might want to be my friend.

I was raised to hate myself, by two people who were raised to hate themselves, by four people who were raised to hate themselves, and so on, I suppose, into infinity. If that sounds like melodrama, I don't mean it to, and I wish I could read the words aloud to you, so that you might hear the dispassion in my tone.

My grandmother died in childbirth with my mother, and so my mother believed, with the kind of belief that transcends all reason, that having a child would be the "death" of her. Her father deserted what remained of the family before the ink on her mother's death certificate was dry—so the family legend goes—and my mother was shipped off to an aunt and uncle who wanted my mother out of the house so badly, they gave her money to run away. At the time of my conception, my father was in love with someone other than my mother, someone he couldn't "live" without, and the fact of my birth deprived him of this other woman's company. In this way, I "killed" both of my parents, and so strong were their own ancient wounds, it was beyond the power of either to forgive me. As a result, I have never had what I would call solidified feelings around things like family and home.

A great deal of the joy I have found in my life I have found while traveling. I have been to sixty countries, the majority of them in Africa and Asia, and there is no doubt that I count the days I spent canoeing in the Okavango Delta in Botswana, trekking to the base camp of Mount Chomolhari in Bhutan, and visiting monasteries during the fall Buddhist festivals all over Asia as the most wonderful days in my life. The men and women I have befriended in Zimbabwe and Laos (to name only a few) are the most wise and compassionate, the most giving and engaging, the most artistically gifted, emotionally centered, the most fully alive people I have ever met. I am utterly happy in places like Namibia and Cambodia, even if I've lost my luggage, even if I am sick with bronchitis and dysentery, even if I'm cold and tired or hot and hungry, even when I haven't seen a familiar face in weeks.

"Ah ha," my therapist always says when I get to this point in the story. "You are far more comfortable loving the unfamiliar, which is a convenient way to avoid loving yourself."

"Fair enough," I always say, and then I go on talking about the pure joy I felt during the monks' debate at the Sera monastery in Tibet.

Intellectually, I can accept his argument, and it is true that although I deeply value the current home I make with my husband and my animals, I have never achieved the level of serenity and satisfaction here that I find in traveling. But I still believe that I would find more people I would want to get to know at, say, a Hmong New Year's celebration on the banks of the Mekong River, than I would, at, say, a home and garden show at the Denver Tech Center. I have spent a good part of my life trying to engage, understand, and learn from all that encompasses the other. And yet, when I look at my life when I am at home on this continent, it pains me to admit that I have very few close friends who are not white, or even friends who were raised in cultural environments that differ very much from my own.

Speaking in the broadest generalities, my father was a racist and my mother was not. We lived in an all-white neighborhood, belonged to an all-white country club, and I attended an all-but-all-white public school. I went to a college that had so few black students that every one of them was a member of the Black Student Union Choir. I've lived the last eleven years in a county in the high mountains of Colorado that has not a single black resident. Before that, I went to graduate school in Salt Lake City, where every time I went to my local health food store, I hoped to run into Karl Malone, the forward for the Utah Jazz, who also shopped there, and who is, in my opinion, the most handsome man on the face of the earth. Now I split my time between Davis, California, and my mountain town, and while Davis would hardly be described as multicultural, it is a definite improvement over Mineral County, Colorado.

I find it curious, and a little troubling, that I have chosen, as an adult, to call some of the whitest places in America home, and have chosen to travel almost exclusively and extensively to countries whose population is largely nonwhite. When I'm traveling, there is nothing that makes me feel better than being accepted—in whatever measure I am—by an Asian or an African person and their family. I find it even more curious and troubling that I haven't made life choices that have allowed me to bring that otherness that I am so drawn to into my life at home.

The other day, I was on the four-minute ride on the Hertz bus between the United terminal at the Sacramento airport and the rental car lot. Sitting across from me was a black man in a black knit shirt and black dress pants. He had large, deeply veined hands; a wide, expressive face; and close-cropped hair. I found it impossible to take my eyes off him, and when he looked up at me, I could feel my stomach turning somersaults. I have never had a visceral attraction of that magnitude to a white man—ever. With a white man it is more likely that I have noticed his good looks, on an almost intellectual level, and only then given him the opportunity to convince me verbally that there was some good reason I should be attracted to him.

Having said all that, it also hurts to admit that I have never acted on my attraction to a black man. I have never had sex with a black man; a black man and I have never shared a kiss. It is also true that I have almost never acted on my attraction to anybody (while I'm on the subject of embarrassing admittances). I have never initiated a first kiss with anyone, never picked up the phone and asked a man out (*Don't ever call a boy*, I can hear my mother screaming from the upstairs bedroom). And so far, in my life, a black man has never made that essential first move on me. It is not outrageous, given the places I have lived, that a black man has never tried to kiss me. It is not outrageous, given my emotional history, that I would feel undeserving if he did.

You might be inclined to dismiss my attraction to black men as some kind of fetish (you might, in fact, be thinking all kinds of terrible things about me by now), but I react to babies almost exactly the same way. I have not had children of my own, and part of the reason is that I find white babies so singularly unappealing. I don't particularly want to hold them, even when protocol suggests that I should. My reticence (and it is more reticence than all-out revulsion) is so strong that I risk offending their mothers in its name. I find black babies, on the other hand, breathtakingly beautiful (and Thai babies, and Bhutanese babies, and Inuit babies), and will go out of my way to hold them. I can spend hours on the Internet adoption pages and fall in love over and over again with kids in orphanages in all corners of the globe.

Most of this, it strikes me, is less about race, and more about self-loathing. The deep kind of self-loathing that might not get in the way of our jobs on a daily basis, or even our marriages, but might leave us waking up one day realizing that *none of my best friends are black*, but not precisely for the reasons most people might think. This is less about race, but maybe more about racism, which always begins, I'd wager, in self-hatred, and from there grows into all of its various and horrifying forms.

I had the amazing good fortune this summer to be chosen by Oprah Winfrey to interview Toni Morrison for *O Magazine*. I didn't, and still don't know why I was chosen, and while I felt many positive emotions going into the interview, thrilled, challenged, excited beyond words, I felt more than anything else, unworthy.

To prepare for the interview, I read (in most cases reread) all of Ms. Morrison's novels. Twice. I vowed not to ask her any questions that I myself don't like to be asked in a similar situation. I prepared no questions in advance to avoid impeding the organic flow of the conversation.

Ms. Morrison spoke a great deal about race and self-loathing, about why the expression "Black is beautiful" was a necessary statement, not only for the whites to hear, but for the blacks to hear about themselves. It is only as I struggle to write this essay that I understand that the reason I have never acted on my attraction to black men, why I am only just now beginning to develop friendships with black women, is a very similar kind of self-loathing. That my feelings of unworthiness around having a black friend—that I am not cool enough, or educated enough in black culture, or simply deserving of the attentions of a race of people I find so much more attractive and interesting and full of wisdom than my own—are maybe not essentially different from those of the guy who says he doesn't have any black friends because he thinks the white race is superior. Somebody told both that guy and me that we were dog shit every day until we believed it. He went to one type of defense mechanism and I to another. It is no coincidence that this is the same kind of lie (you are dog shit) that white-dominated culture has been telling black people for hundreds of years. It is not news to me that racism begins in self-hatred. What has been startling about writing this essay is discovering that to identify this phenomenon, I need look no farther than myself.

About two hours into the interview, Ms. Morrison said, "I'm going upstairs for a minute, but I'm going to ask you a question, and when I come down you can give me your answer. Several people have told me that *Love* is my most accessible book so far. Can you tell me what they mean by that?" And then she went upstairs.

I had stayed up all the night before to read *Love* for the third time. I could have practically recited passages from it. When she came back downstairs, I said, "They don't mean *more accessible*. What they mean is *less hard on the white peo-*

*ple.*" Which, I imagine for more complicated reasons than I will ever understand, made the great Toni Morrison smile.

When you add the slipperiness of language to the already unstable slope of a white woman talking about race and racism, an avalanche can't be too far behind, and it is amazing how all day today even my best intentions continue to get it wrong. There isn't a sentence I have written that I don't want to qualify, take back, rearticulate. There hasn't been a moment of writing this essay that I haven't imagined all the ways you, my various imagined readers, must be thinking badly of me.

What I want most to tell you—what I am most afraid to tell you, is that Toni Morrison liked me; that a two-hour interview turned into lunch, and then into dinner. That we talked about bathroom fixtures and Italian shoes and Kobe Bryant and O. J. Simpson. That once I made her laugh so hard that she threw herself sideways into a chair. That instead of seeing a scared white girl who would never understand her, her racial experience, or her artistic vision, she saw someone who was worthy of her time and attention, and she gave those things to me with more generosity than I could have ever dreamed possible. What I want most to tell you is that that gift has changed my life.

Why? Because I believe that she is the greatest living writer. Because her writing methods and philosophies are enough like mine that they give me something to strive for. Because she talked about teaching with such passion that I will take that passion with me every time I step into a classroom for the rest of my life. Because she is black? I don't know the answer. It is an exercise in stupidity (at best) to imagine how I would feel if she were white. She is black, she is the greatest living writer, she is Toni Morrison. If she were here now, she might remind me that *that* may be the point.

It was a few weeks after the interview that I met Abigail in Provincetown. On the last night there, several of us played a game called I've Never, where you say a sentence that begins with those words—"I've never spent a night in jail," or "I've never had sex with a complete stranger"—and those who have done either of those things must lift their glasses, thereby identifying themselves as transgressors, and drink. We were all more or less heterosexuals approaching mid-life, and when a man in the group named Frank said, "I've never had sex with a man," only the women picked up their glasses. Obviously, none of the other men had had a homosexual experience, either.

That led to a conversation about sex, as is often the case in the game I've Never. A man named Jason said that sometimes he wished he were gay, because it was his observation, at least in Provincetown, that gay men seemed a lot more interested in having a lot more sex than the women he knew—his wife, for example—and the other men in the room agreed, a little too heartily.

Without so much as a glance at each other, Abigail and I made a mutual decision to relieve those men of their outdated misconception. Abigail is Ivy League–educated, and I loved listening to her enumerate the evidence against the faulty premise—that men like to have sex more than women—as if she were giving a talk at a Modern Language Association conference. I supported her with personal and anecdotal evidence, and by the time we were finished, the men in the room were convinced that Abigail, me, and all of our girlfriends were having more sex in a week than they had in a year. To hear us tell it, there has never been a group of women on earth who have as much sex as we do. In that swirl of argument and enthusiasm, Abigail and I were anything but two women of different races. We were one well-practiced debate team, one set of libidinous urges, one woman, one voice.

I was, in that argument—if not outright lying—exaggerating a great deal, and I feel sure that Abigail was, too, in spite of the fact that we are two people who are often accused—if anything—of being too honest. I believe we stretched the truth a little, not to make the men feel bad, or even to make ourselves feel good by cracking over our bare, summertime knees that old saw we have seen on one too many sitcoms. We did it, I believe, to declare our friendship to each other. To say, I have seen how smart and articulate and sexy and beautiful you are, and I will fight this meaningless little battle side by side with you, just to prove it.

Here is what change is: A forty-year-old white woman lives around white people all her life. One black woman says, *As it turns out, you are worthy,* and the white woman believes it enough to turn around and say it to somebody else. On all sides are the sounds of doors and windows opening.

# AS MY FRIEND
# ZACHARY SAYS KADDISH
# FOR HIS FATHER...

## Darryl Pinckney

As my friend Zachary says Kaddish for his father, I think back some thirty-seven years to one Friday afternoon in June 1967, and our eighth grade American history class at Westlane Junior High School in Indianapolis, Indiana. Zach and I sat across from each other. We competed to see who could score higher on tests. That Friday afternoon, everyone seemed extraordinarily happy. The school year was nearly over. The teacher stepped from the room. This was an "accelerated class"; he wasn't always needed. As soon as the door closed, paper airplanes emerged from notebooks, their bases, and took flight. Most of the planes sailing up toward the combat zone of fluorescent lights had the Star of David on their wings. It was like Cowboys and Indians. Most everyone wanted to be a cowboy. Few wanted to draw the Crescent. Zach never acted up in class, but this time was different. He was joining in and being very aerodynamic with his paper construction, so much so that he hadn't finished his careful folding by the time the teacher returned. I hadn't known until that class that a war was going on in the Middle East. I was avoiding my parents and their evening news, their papers. A black kid in a mostly white school, I kept my ignorance to myself and picked up what I could from the joy. Everywhere, Israel was winning. What would be known, over here, as the Six-Day War was coming to its close. We gathered up our books, and Zach explained the meaning of the Star of David. Oh. He gave me his plane.

Summer interrupted this new friendship, this addition to my education. Zach went with his family to upstate New York, where they had a place that Zach complained meant weeks of more chores than fun. When school began again in the fall, he had grown taller and darker and was taking more "accelerated" classes than anyone. Though Zach and I had no classes to- gether anymore, we'd become friends. In those waning days of the Great Society, we, the black students, the integrators, knew which of our white school friends were real friends, because they came to our houses and we went to theirs. Only years later would it occur to me that most of them were Jewish. I rode bicycles with new friends through wheat fields that are now complexes of garden apartments and suburban churches. Mothers made huge sandwiches. From the Journalism Club I learned that not all Jewish people went to the same kind of temple, or to temple at all. Some Jewish families went skiing or boating as the high holy days approached. School awards for perfect attendance never went to a Jewish student. But for me, Zach's family, his Polish mother, his descended-from-pogrom father, his long-haired older brother, smart little brother, and smart little sister—for me, that family was from Europe, or New York. They spoke and thought as though they were from someplace else, had been somewhere else, and that made all the difference.

In Indianapolis, every tribe had its own place. The rich whites had their tree-shrouded enclaves; the poor whites had their side of town; and the Catholics in between had their own high schools and formidable basketball teams. We, black and Protestant, had our churches in town, back in the neighborhoods we'd moved out of; and the People of the Book, as my increasingly unbalanced grandfather called them when he visited, had their temples. The polling station my parents went to back then was located in the segregated country club just across the street from us. There were no Jews among its members, never mind blacks. Maybe it's changed by now. As more blacks moved not far from us into an area dubbed the Golden Ghetto, the polling station also migrated—to the local firehouse. However, anyone, they said, was made welcome at the Jewish Community Center. It offered an Israeli Folk Dancing Club, which was great fun, and special programs related to Yom HaShoa, Holocaust Remembrance Day. One evening, I came away with a copy of Elie Wiesel's *Night* and read it in one sitting. I didn't mention to anyone how much the part about the young people making love in the sealed death train stuck in my mind. I stepped up from Chaim Potok to Bernard Malamud and fell back again. I began to keep a diary after I read Anne Frank. We saw the film; some group staged the play. One girl was nearly as good at being selfish and irritating as Shelley Winters.

The first time I visited a temple, I thought the board of names with a small bulb beside each commemorated victims of the Holocaust. The board was commemorative in its function—Yahrzeit—but the numbers were the dates of deaths according to the Hebrew calendar, not the concentration camp numbers I'd read about. Though I read a little book called *What the Jews Believe*, conversion never crossed my mind, just as a wish to convert me was never present in the tone of my Jewish friends when they answered my casual questions. We didn't talk about Israel or the Middle East. Israel's right to exist was a given among liberals. The burning issues— race, the Vietnam War—were on the homefront. Only a year after its proclamation in Haight-Ashbury, the Summer of Love was already a memory, though politics seemed as far away as the big cities I dreamed of living in. It perhaps meant a great deal to parents, white and black, that their children got along, shared a common language, that of being young, especially when Indianapolis joined the list of places where riots broke out as night descended over the news that Martin Luther King had been assassinated. Senator Kennedy was in town for a campaign appearance and went into the inner city in an attempt to speak to the anger. Two months later, he, too, was gunned down.

The country was changing, and, once in high school, so were we. The violence at the Democratic Party's national convention in Chicago in the summer of 1968 had made radicals of many formerly nice boys and girls and even some youngish or bachelor teachers. The politics that once seemed far away turned out to be as near as older siblings in college, as near as the suddenly sophisticated at the next table in the school library, who complained that books relevant to their needs would never be on the shelves. The inflammatory rhetoric of Black Power translated at our sprawling, super-equipped high school, with its parking lot for juniors and another for seniors, into a separate table for black students in the cafeteria. The anti–Vietnam War movement fed the general wish to oppose the authority of principals and out-of-it teachers. The days of the battle between us and them. I say "us," though most of the political discussions that engaged my peers were over my head.

Zach got his driver's license that spring, and to help me with an assignment for the school newspaper, he took me into the city, to the home of the black poet Mari Evans. I just assumed she'd be a black separatist and made him wait in the car, though he was the one who'd read *Soul on Ice* in his free time. My interests ran toward Antonia Fraser. Evans was generous, but Zach would have asked her better questions.

We noticed that things were getting weird, not yet knowing what such a phrase could mean. Meanwhile, Zach's father, a doctor and a professor of medicine, was taking his family with him for his year's sabbatical at the Weizmann Institute in Rehovoth, Israel. I see so clearly an afternoon picnic of farewell: my father, my mother, Zach's father and mother, Zach's brothers and his sister. And their aunt Robie, a filmmaker from New York, a professor of film from New York University. She was going to sneak Zach and his older brother to New York's Lower East Side, to the Electric Circus, a rock-'n'-roll venue I'd heard of from album cover notes. I remember asking Zach's mother if she planned to keep a kosher kitchen in Israel and then being surprised by the work that keeping kosher entailed for her. "Kosher" was a word I'd strayed across. When the Journalism Club met in various homes, one kid always passed on the trays of shrimp. But the dairy thing, the pots and pans thing, the chicken thing. And Zach's mother baked. It was so Old World. Back then, the South was our Old World. As we drove off, my father raved about Zach's mother's cakes. My mother said that there were enough black women who were known for being good cooks, she didn't have to be one of them. My father said Zach and his siblings were all brilliant, like their father. And like their mother, my mother added.

Later that summer, when I was reading Hesse and watching World War II documentaries, my father brought home a package he'd taken to the post office to open in front of an inspector. He laughed as he put the box on the table. The parcel had come from Turkey. We certainly didn't know anyone in Turkey. In those days, when drugs were becoming more than feature stories, when drugs could very well have been as close as the park where Indianapolis's hippies and freaks liked to gather in good weather, my father didn't want to take any chances. Inside the box, under the newspaper, were two candlesticks, a present to us from Zach's mother. His family had made their way to Israel by way of London and had evidently visited Turkey as well. That was so nice of her, my mother said. Sometimes, back then, when to be black in a "predominantly white school" meant that you were cool even if you weren't, white friends would eventually get around to the heart-to-heart talk in which they examined, for you, their thoughts and feelings about knowing a black "personally" for the first time. But Zach's older brother ran around with a black girl who had a reputation at our high school for being extremely intelligent and dangerously wild. His family knew more than one black family. I was not a social experiment, an occasion for reflections on race.

It was the year that Zach was away in Israel that round-table discussions on race relations came into vogue at our high school. To listen to white parents insist that Martin Luther King had been an agent of communist governments was, we were assured, to do our part in the "war on apathy." But the lines were hardening all around us, thanks to Nixon's Southern strategy. I went to one or two meetings of a group that Zach had been closely associated with, Students for Democratic Action, our high school's necessarily milder version of Students for a Democratic Society, the notorious SDS. The threat of the draft and the call of youth's music broke down tribal barriers. Some WASPs wanted in. The more brutal the conservative reaction, nationally and locally, to the forces of change, the more important it was for "us" to band together, regardless of where we'd come from. By the time ordinary black women in Indianapolis were refusing to accept the flag at the funerals of their soldier sons, a newspaper clipping had come from Israel, showing Zach getting his high school diploma from Golda Meir. He would not be coming back to our high school. He was already off to college.

Zach was a bearded freshman at Indiana University and could quote at length from Fireside Theater skits and Woody Allen films. He had stories of girls, Rome, Amsterdam. He had a Volvo, but he was still tone deaf when he sang along to the car radio. I was a high school senior who always needed a ride, who never had wheels, because I didn't have a driver's license, and wouldn't be getting one any time soon, because twice I'd driven without a license, and had a serious accident. I knew much more about why Zach and his brothers did not go in for the Volkswagen Day-Glo vans that were so popular at the time, why his family would not buy a German-made car, why my enthusiasm for German literature didn't seem to come up. There was too much to talk about to wonder about the subjects we just didn't get around to when we met on his college breaks. It was the season of weird stuff.

In his bell bottoms and T-shirt and James Taylor–style country vest, Zach was as serious about science as ever. When I finally joined him on the Indiana University campus in the limestone country of Bloomington, Indiana, Zach was starting his second year, but he was already a senior. Then, a few dorm parties and exams later, he was gone to graduate school at Cornell, in snowbound, isolated, suicidal-making Ithaca, New York, and I'd packed my love for Angela Davis and transferred to Columbia. To be a student there was the only way I could get my parents to let me marry the streets of New York. I don't remember what Zach and I said about Tricky Dick, the tragedy of the Munich Olympics, McGovern, or the Yom Kippur War, but we must have said something about these things when he came to visit me in New York City. But, then, I also don't remember a drop of what his Ph.D. was about. I do remember we went with his aunt Robie to see *Hester Street*, a marvelous film, and she laughed that I could pretend to get the Yiddish. And of course I want to bring down the curtain right away on drunken summer scenes: the twenty-first birthday parties and who threw up in whose car and who wore the trashcan on his head all night and whose mother made apologies to whose mother when the suffering party was collected the morning after.

How have the years gone by? They have labels, like snapshot captions: Zach back in Indianapolis in medical school; Zach and Judy married; Zach and Judy in Baltimore; birth of their first daughter; Zach and Judy again in Indianapolis; birth of their second daughter. I moved to Europe, but whenever I went back to Indianapolis to see my family, I would also see Zach, the Christmas Jew, as he called himself, because he was always on call at that time of year. There were new stories to go with the old feelings. Friendship can travel, can spread among members of families. My sisters thought of Zach and his bearded brothers, "the Furry Freak Brothers," as their friends, too. Zach's parents turned up at our weddings, we at theirs, at fiftieth anniversary celebrations, at the bat mitzvahs of grand-daughters. The next thing I knew, a photograph of Zach and his family at the upstate New York home they were selling off included his parents, his brothers, his sister, their spouses, and his parents' nine grandchildren.

I leave it to my father to remark that of all the white people he's met in Indianapolis over the years, the ones he has the most respect for are "the Jews." He firmly believes that self-made men share a common language. I leave it to my father to be the towering figure in my memory of visits during which his long disquisition on various aspects of race and black history careened into awkward scenes of his appreciation of "the Jews" as a people who know how to stick together, how to take care of their own. "We" should emulate them more, he said. But then he also approves of Edith Piaf for the same reason: She said that after you make it to the top, you're supposed to send the elevator back down.

From praise of "the Jews" for their tribal cohesion, he moved into praise of their diasporic heroes, their secular stars: Marx, Einstein, Freud. Menuhin, my mother once added.

197

Barbra Streisand, my sister said, rolling her eyes at me. And then Zach wouldn't know what to say when my father said it did not surprise him at all that Zach and his brothers turned out to be brilliant physicians. Historically, Jews had to be brilliant, my father insisted, because they could only be of the city. We had to hear, again, how my father and his brother, students, arrived in New York on their way to summer work on the tobacco farms in Connecticut. They had cardboard suitcases and not enough money to check them. Later, they could afford to go to "the Jews," that is, to shop in Harlem. Then my father would explain, again, what Langston Hughes meant by his title *Fine Clothes to the Jews*, and the experience he was describing. We squirmed some more.

How would Richard Wright and James Baldwin have got started—noticed—without "the Jews" in the Communist Party, "the Jews" and their intellectual quarterlies? The social alliances came from political alliances, but even then the world of Chester Himes's fraught Black-Jewish Party romances was not for everyone. Georgia has the Negro and Harlem has the Jew, Baldwin says in an essay from the 1950s, thinking about some of the resentments that contributed to the Harlem riots of 1935, 1943. By the time of Baldwin's essay, "the Jews" no longer lived in Harlem; only their businesses remained. But the Jewish students among the Freedom Riders were the children of the Jewish radicalism of the Depression era, just as the recent memoirs of growing up both black and Jewish constitute part of the legacy of the Freedom Riders and the civil rights days of acting out your principles in real human terms.

To grow up in the 1960s was to come of age in the last days

of the black-Jewish coalition. After television journalists found the parents of one of the murdered civil rights volunteers in Mississippi and the father said how proud he was of his dead son, it never occurred to me that "the Jews" were not on my side or that I was not on theirs. Some articles from the 1960s people were still debating in the 1970s. Norman Podhoretz's "My Negro Problem—and Ours," reads mostly as a whine about the bullies from his school days, which I can understand. Better Mailer's frank, challenging admiration of Bebop and the hipster. But in some campus circles in the early 1970s, Harold Cruse's *The Crisis of the Negro Intellectual* was an item on a bill of indictment. Cruse is incandescent at the thought of what Jewish influence in the party did to hinder the development of useful theories of black nationalism. I remember opening a copy of this book in someone's dorm room and seeing "Fuck You Jew" scrawled across a page. The same bookshelf held Jason Epstein's *The Great Conspiracy Trial*, with its Jewish judge ordering a black militant defendant in the trial of the Chicago Seven chained and gagged.

Maybe the black-Jewish coalition began to fall apart in New York, with the teachers' strike and the Brownsville–Ocean Hill mess. I remember the night the Jewish Defense League was born on the Columbia University campus in 1975. I can't listen to a settler ranting on the West Bank without thinking back to those guys in yarmulkes in close formation, chanting in front of Ferris Booth Hall, their fists raised to the night and a few tipped-off cameras. They looked like losers who had become important by being as unreasonable as everyone else who was running around in those days. They looked like people who hadn't yet declared their major, doing an imitation of the Black Panthers, a copycat moment Mailer could not have predicted.

In the late 1970s, in New York, capital of the Jewish Diaspora, it was still somewhat possible to think the black-Jewish coalition existed when needed. But then came the Reagan years and neo-conservative exasperation with the prestige of liberal culture and the supposed ingratitude of blacks. Then came the stigma of the underclass and the murders in Crown Heights, Brooklyn. Zach and I could both shake our heads at Farrakhan, but we—I—had avoided the subject of Sharon's invasion of Lebanon. We could shake our heads at the poor scholarship of Leonard Jeffries at City College and Tony Martin at Wellesley. Then, in the late 1980s, I moved to Berlin. Zach ribbed me for it on my holiday visits to Indianapolis. We sang "Springtime for Hitler" a lot, with me struggling not to follow Zach off key. And just when I thought we couldn't talk about the intifada, we did. Yes, something had to be done.

In 1993, I went to a showing of *Schindler's List* with Zach and his parents in Indianapolis. Beepers went off and the elderly behind us exclaimed at what they recognized of Krakow. Afterward, everyone was very subdued. Not the setting in which to complain about the red coat and Spielberg's sentimentality no matter the film; not the right time to observe that Lanzmann's *Shoah*, with his ability to interview survivors in their own languages, is the greater work. I didn't even want to say that I was surprised to see on screen someone I knew, an actress from Berlin. Zach's mother was there at the movie only because she and her mother were in London in 1939. Her

mother had a cold and couldn't take the scheduled plane back
to Poland, because in those days cabins weren't pressurized.
Zach's mother once said that she spent the war sitting in hotel
lobbies, making up stories to herself about people. Zach and
I still had the intifada to shake our heads and beards over.
Something had to be done. Best, however, not to broach the
subject in Aunt Robie's presence. She dropped out of Vassar
in 1948 and found herself helping to man a radar station
during the 1948 war in the British mandate of Palestine. She
was transferred, because instead of looking for enemy planes,
she'd been tracking buses in Haifa. Best to let the story end
there. Aunt Robie is unafraid of her opinions. "I hate Ethel
Rosenberg," she who used to attend a Trotskyite summer camp
said. But the jokes are over.

Now we walk with new absences in our lives, Zach, my old
friend, and I. In the aftermath of September 11, 2001, I was
struck by the fatalism among some Jewish friends. Israel would
be thrown over; it's always easy to dump "the Jews." People
can't wait to turn on the Jews, the hidden feeling seemed to be.
But Zach was angry. It was Christmas; he was still going to
temple for his father, who had died suddenly in September.
Tragedy stood behind tragedy. I'd never seen or heard Zach so
furious. Give them their state and put up a wall, he raged.
They left their land. But how can anyone trust Arafat.
Meanwhile, in the United States, out in the Midwest, at least,
Arabs had become, for blacks, the new Koreans. There is little
solidarity among blacks and Arabs in such places, though the
two groups share the problem of being the focus of "racial pro-
filing" among the security forces. Blacks can be scathing about
the Arabs—and about Indians (the subcontinent variety), too,

for that matter. Who will come after the blacks have followed the Patimkins to the suburbs?—Neil wonders as he surveys the decayed street from the steps of the Newark Public Library in *Goodbye, Columbus*.

The road forks. Islamic extremism, Christian fundamentalism, Zionist fury, Hindu nationalism—religious intolerance and the politics of hatred offend cultural and familial values, but the road divides as two friends become reluctant to connect the horror of September 11 to the bloodshed in Israel and Palestine. I want to understand. Zach has more in common with the educated, thoughtful refuseniks, the Israeli soldiers who don't want to serve on the West Bank, than he does with the snarling settlers. I want to say that his mother's family didn't die so that her people could preside over apartheid in Judea. I want to say something like that, but I am afraid of offending a rare and good soul. I tell myself that I can't understand what it means, in much the same way that white friends used to admit they'd never know what race means, because they couldn't climb inside the skin of the discriminated against. But some of them could—and should now again, perhaps. I want to say such things, but the anxiety I saw in Zach's eyes the last time we talked goes back too far, back to Poland, Russia, back to a history, to the question of whose history.

Zach is my friend and I am his pal. When I next call, to explain why I did not appear in June to take his daughters to the Indiana State Fair as promised, I will maybe have a chance to mention that the Palestinian activist Hanan Ashrawi called for the suicide bombers to stop. I am relieved to find my private opinions pegged to her public statements, like a weak currency riding a stronger one in the gone world of the gold standard. Yes, I do trust that Zach and I have common ground. I love his family and he loves mine. My mother likes to remember that when I had an emergency appendectomy in Indianapolis in 1980, Zach's father beat her and my father to my bedside the morning after the operation. He was a kind and intelligent man. We have so many things to talk about, Zach and I: families, work, middle age, our shared past, the days of our youth when we could sing "Give Peace a Chance" loudly or talk about Simone Weil's essay "The *Iliad*, Poem of Might":

> *The death of Hector was to give but short-lived joy to Achilles and the death of Achilles brief joy to the Trojans, and the annihilation of Troy but brief joy to the Achaians . . .*

# WITH ME WHERE I GO

## Somini Sengupta

Dear Joe,

For months after you'd gone, your watch, the plastic one your daddy gave you because you were always late, would bleep randomly. It was a short, piercing bleep. Sometimes it went off at nine in the morning, sometimes at midnight. Friends were spooked by it. An itinerant lover once jumped. I thought of it as your heartbeat. How can I know exactly when it stopped? I can tell you only that it was one day in summer. In between the silence of my breath and the asthmatic morning wheeze of the coffee machine, sometime after the early evening jingle of the ice cream truck down below and the fury of teenage lovers airing their grievances on the stoop across the way, their chins jutting in petulance long past midnight, I noticed your watch had turned quiet and cold.

We had barely met that first time we got caught up in a brawl. We argued until light came up in the sky. I sat on your dirty clothes hamper. I could smell my funky breath. I was afraid you'd notice. Smelly Indian. You pointed a long, pretty finger at me. I noticed: no gunk under your nails. Your words came flying at me, furiously.

Negroes died for the right to vote is what you said. You haven't even made an investment in this motherfucker.

(Forgive me, baby, for committing this to paper. It's humiliating to recall our spats now. But there's a sweetness to it that says everything about how maddening and vital it was to be your friend.)

Our argument was ostensibly about why I hadn't bothered to become an American citizen, to "naturalize," as it's called. I carried an Indian passport, even though I hadn't lived in India since I was seven years old. Truth be told, I'd been too lazy to go through the mechanics: the fingerprints and fees and the submission of one form after another. You know how supremely disorganized I am about such things. But I had highfalutin reasons, too, as I passionately declared that night. I would not pledge to take up arms for this motherfucker, I told you. I had dreamed of going to Cuba and being embraced as a Third World sister. I didn't see the need to go to polls and have to choose, year after year, between dumb and dumber. I must have called you parochial. You must have called me ignorant. Our eyes must have turned bloodred from fighting. We must have been babies. We must have wanted to be known, really known. Why else would we have carried on like this?

It's a wonder we held on as long as we did. We brawled famously, about everything. But it was the subject of citizenship, or some variation on that theme (from why the cabdriver hates the Negro to why Dominicans send their money home instead of keeping it here), that we would return to, again and again, circling round like two men in a ring, jabbing, jumping, holding each other by the neck for dear mercy. We played our parts: native vs. alien, colored vs. colored, clan vs. clan.

Our clans needed each other. Yours needed mine to remind themselves they belonged on this soil. Mine needed yours to know who was on top and who was at bottom. It's the immigrant's rite of passage.

And then, under the epidermis of our public identities, there was you and me. Somewhere in the foul brown muck of our antagonism was a more primal longing. Did you hear me trying to tell you, "Tell me about, show me, who am I?"

Did you hear me? Did I hear you? You always talked in such soft mumbles.

"S," you write one morning while I sleep. "Don't I hold you like a feather?"

To write, they tell us, is to wage war against forgetting. To write is to save that which would otherwise vanish. Like you, up a treacherous mountain one morning, then vanished, presumed dead. 1964–1999. You can't live if you can't remember, they say. But you can't live if you can't forget, no? Writing this, I am remembering us, arguing the world. I am remembering us, prying each other open, standing naked in absolute terror. But maybe I am also forgetting. Maybe I am remembering myself. Maybe I am hoping to be remembered, so that I won't lose myself again.

When we first meet, it is not your face I notice, not your hands, not your soft middle. I notice your voice. We are in a noisy crowd. I strain to hear you. We stand on the edge of a dance floor, and we whisper to each other. We talk about dark and fair. We talk about family. You're being a hound dog, and I know it. But I stand closer and closer, wanting to hear you better, wanting to hear you more. I learn later that you are fully capable of yelling at the top of your lungs. But the mumbles are your way of pulling people in, banishing chitchat, demanding an intimacy that is disarming and rare in the circles we move in. Everyone claims you as their best friend, when you're gone. I have fallen into the same trap, I suppose. Death allows us to possess the past completely.

The first time I cross the Mason-Dixon line, I am with you. I tell you I'm scared of the American South. You tell me I've been overfed George Wallace clichés. I relent easily. The South is your America. It is our first holiday together, and I am safe. In Savannah, a stranger insists on taking our picture. We are sitting on a stoop of an antebellum house. It has a green door. We are happy and a little fat from being in love. I am looking up at your eyes and I am giggling so hard, the pictures come out a little blurry. When do babies learn to do that? To look at someone else's eyes? We wander from one old church to another, and you scribble in your spiral notebook, back curved like a question mark. We wander around an old cemetery where you think some of your people might be buried, and a black man, maybe your daddy's age, his hair straighter than mine, his nose hawkish, squints at me and says, "You from around here? No? You look like your people could be from around here." I catch your smile.

You go back South many times to inquire after your family's story. Once, on a trip to Birmingham, your daddy's hometown, you cart back a plastic ice bucket full of Alabama dirt, the color of sweet potato, baked. You keep the ice bucket near your feet, next to your desk, in the study. Was it a Holiday Inn ice bucket? You always had a preference for Holiday Inn. You sit in the study in woolly socks and long johns, winter and summer and everything in between, slurping orange juice, your dirty glasses falling down your nose, and the ice bucket stays at your feet, next to your desk.

Years later, after you're gone, I return to Alabama. I am there to write an article about a proposed landfill on the Selma-to-Montgomery highway, not far from Birmingham. Here, in 1965, MLK led his most famous march for black franchise. Sharecroppers who dared to register to vote were tossed off their land. A civil rights worker, a Detroit housewife named Viola Luozzo, was gunned down here. Today, predictably, the thought of a landfill on such hallowed ground inspired impassioned, polarized opinions, and it's not just along black-white lines. Some see it as an engine of economic growth, others as an affront to history. Garbage vs. memory: It's the sort of story you would like. Naturally, you are with me in my rented Pontiac as I drive along this empty four-lane highway on a hot October afternoon. And you point out the obvious. On the banks of the highway are miles and miles of your red Alabama dirt, millions of ice buckets' worth. I roll down the windows and I stick out my tongue. I can taste you.


The first time you and I go to California to visit my family, we stop off at a spa in the hills north of San Francisco. We are drawn by what we've heard about the place. They serve healthy vegetarian food. We can swim and hike, get a massage and a tour of the vineyards on the way back.

When we get there, midday in the middle of May, we find not one but five natural spring pools, each of different temperature. We put down our backpacks, pull on our swimsuits. Only when we wander over to the pools and look closely at our fellow guests do we realize where we are: a nudie colony for neo-hippies. We are the only colored people here.

We go native, strip down and slip into the water. We swim from hot to lukewarm to frigid. I try not to look at you. You've got your lips pursed, swallowing a smirk. No one looks at us. No one talks to us. At dinnertime, it's the same. The dining room is a gallery of Guatemalan-weave baggy pants and Balinese print sarongs. The meals, too, are of the crunchy granola variety: greens and tamari, brown rice, soy milk for coffee. We try to make eye contact with other guests. No luck. You ask me, "How can you wander around naked all day, looking at pink weenies, and then not even say, 'Hi'?" The next morning you are up early. I find you outside, admiring one of our neighbors. She is topless. Her breasts are perky and pink. Her eyes are closed, and she is sitting in lotus position, chanting, "Om." You giggle soundlessly when I give you a dirty look.

We pull into my parents' house late that evening, woozy from sun and Chardonnay tastings. At the dinner table, my mother warns you that she'll eat with her hands, and then issues this strange missive, practically her first words to you. "We are very Bengali," she says, referring to herself and my father, noticeably leaving me out. "Very Bengali." Throughout the rest of dinner, she talks about a boy called Kwame who, we gather, is black, and who has been to the house lately for a film project with my sister. "Kwame likes this food, too," my mother announces. Then, "The dog barks at you just like she barks at Kwame." Then, "Kwame also went to Yale." The next morning, I find you and my mother in hushed conversation at the kitchen table. I am alarmed, even a little upset. What could you possibly be talking about? Neither of you will say, not even now. But whatever it is, it banishes forever the lecture I'd been expecting to hear from my mother, something about "our culture" and "their culture." Instead, after we come home, she tells me she loves you because I love you. It doesn't take her long to send pictures of us back to the family in Calcutta. You're my "special friend," she writes. And that you went to Yale.

These days, my mother keeps a Robert Johnson postcard you once sent tacked up to her dressing table mirror. She talks about you only when she thinks I'm out of earshot. Last Christmas, I caught her ladling rice pudding into small glass bowls and whispering to my aunt, "He liked this so much."


Some weeks after the planes have rammed into the Twin Towers, I am talking to a clutch of young men playing ball at a Brooklyn park. They are high school students. All but one, who is the child of Salvadoran immigrants, are black. Oh yes, things have changed, they say. The shopkeepers no longer trail them 24/7. The police don't hound them. Instead, they stop the men who look "Middle Eastern." (What does a Middle Eastern look like? Ralph Nader? My friend's father, a retired New Jersey engineer who wears a turban?) The boys tell me they're still too rattled to get on the subway, especially in neighborhoods where there are lots of "Middle Easterners." "The first thing that's running through my mind is, Does he have a bomb strapped on him just wait for it to go off?" one of them says. "I mean, you don't know who's who anymore," another confesses. "It kinda makes you think, Is this person for America or against America? And if they're against America, what can they do?"

I'm in reporter mode. I listen. I prod. I hope what they're telling me approximates what they're feeling in their hearts. Would they feel differently, I wonder, if you were standing by me?

The question of citizenship has slapped us in the face since September 11. Record numbers have applied for naturalization, crushing an already beleaguered federal immigration agency. American flags are hoisted everywhere. My neighbors, two elderly West Indian women, have one dangling from the second-floor window. Drive through Washington Heights or the heart of Caribbean central Brooklyn: the symbols of the Dominican Republic, Haiti, and Jamaica have taken a backseat to the Stars-and-Stripes. Cabdrivers have slapped American flag stickers on their back windows. Balbir Singh Sodhi, a Sikh man who ran a Chevron station in a suburb of Phoenix, Arizona, had apparently asked his brother to buy a flag to hoist at his station. Too bad for him, Stars-and-Stripes were sold out that week. Balbir Singh Sodhi was planting flowers outside his gas station on the Saturday after September 11 when a man pulled up in a pick-up truck and shot and killed him. A local newspaper reported that when he was arrested by police later that day, Balbir Sing Sodhi's assailant yelled, "I'm a patriot. I'm an American. I'm a damn American all the way." In the following weeks, Sikhs poured out into the streets. They held vigils and marches in Washington, New York, Phoenix. They wore red-white-and-blue turbans and they held up homemade placards, as if beseeching the ignorant: "We [heart] America." Should it have moved me? It only made my blood boil.

Black people get to be American at times like this. Double consciousness can take a holiday. Why not? It's so rare. A poll in New Jersey, conducted in the weeks after September 11, asked if airport officials should regard Middle Eastern travelers with "more suspicion" than others. Among blacks, thirty-eight percent said yes; among whites, forty-two percent. Nor did black and white answers differ much on the question of whether immigration from the Middle East should be more restrictive: twenty-nine percent of blacks and twenty-three percent of whites said it should be halted, while fifty-five percent of blacks and fifty-six percent of whites said it should be limited. I hear that an Indian woman, a corporate type on the Boston–New York train, is pulled off and interrogated on the platform. A Pakistani on his way to a family wedding is thrown off a flight because his fellow passengers are afraid. ("Flying while brown" is the name of this hazard). An Indian woman, smart, passionate, world-traveled, tells me: "Now we know what it feels like to be black." Really? Where were we, I wonder, when it was "driving while black"?

It is with some relief that I read John Edgar Wideman's essay in *Harper's* some months later. It is the closest I come to having a conversation with you. "I'm sorry. I'm an American of African descent and I can't applaud my president for doing unto foreign others what he's inflicted on me and mine," Wideman writes. "I'm sorry. It's too late. I can't be as good an American as he's telling me to be."

He continues: "If you promote all the surviving Afghans to the status of honorary Americans, Mr. President, where exactly on the bus does that leave me?" There it is again, baby: the native's claim. What would you have said to those boys in the park, I wonder. Their America is your America, too.

I am sitting on a beach, an empty, two-mile stretch of sand on the Caribbean, waiting for turtles. The mother turtle will hatch her eggs here. Then she will chase her babies off the beach and into the sea, knowing a great many of them won't make it. The ones who live will remember the beach where they were born forever. They will swim across the ocean one day and come back. My words fall on the page like the newborn turtles running unwittingly into the abyss.

Do you remember? Some years ago, for entirely unprincipled reasons, because I had had it with the indignities of traveling with an Indian passport, I relented and applied for citizenship. The application contains a long list of yeses and no's. No, I'm not a communist. Yes, I will bear arms for the defense of the United States of America. On the day of my interview, the occasion that makes real foreigners quiver, I drive to a squat beige warehouse on Long Island, pass through a phalanx of surly West Indian guards, wait in a room with dirty blue carpet until Rebecca, my interviewer, comes to get me. She is a large woman, one shade lighter than you, and she sweats when she walks and has trouble getting through doorways. She is cheerful and irreverent, a temp who's been hired to help out with

the backlog in naturalizations. Among the ten "civic" questions she asks me is "Who is Martin Luther King?" I ask her
how long that question has been part of the exam. She shrugs.
She couldn't care less. She got the job answering an ad in the
paper. She gets no benefits. She figures she'll be out of work in
another few months. She likes that I'm a newspaperwoman.
She tells me to write a story about a coworker, a West Indian
who looks a lot like me and who peeks into her office from time
to time and throws lint balls. She likes him, I can tell.

On the morning I am to be sworn in, I wake up late, hung
over and reeking of a delightfully stinky Italian cheese I'd eaten
for dinner the night before. Smelly Indian. The benches in the
courthouse are jam-packed by the time I arrive. There is no
room to take off our coats, so we all keep them on, the room
steamy with our sweat. The Bengali on one side has that ubiq-
uitous onion-ginger-cumin-coriander scent on hers. On the
other side sits someone who's eaten a root vegetable the night
before, a turnip maybe. The Chinese in front of me smell like
bulletproof chicken wings.

The courtroom is dimly lit. Portraits of white-haired, white-
skinned men hang on one wall. Chaos prevails for a long time.
A great many of my comrades speak no English, and the room
is so crowded that their handlers and translators must wait out
in the hall. A beaming Sikh has on a bright blue turban and a
red-white-and-blue tie. A backbent Russian has stowed all his
documents under his furry cap. It seems no one can or wants
to follow directions, which seems to send a thick-necked INS
officer's blood pressure soaring. He barks: "What part of NO
don't you understand?" Or, "Let's do this like we're in the fifth
grade, shall we?" I imagine you would have said something

snarky about how these people learn to hate the Negro before they learn to speak English, and I imagine we would have had a knock-down drag-out.

For three hours, I wait. I sit. I stand in a line to dump my green card (they are incinerated, I am told). I wait some more. The ceremony begins when the judge walks in, and suddenly the INS officer near me is a picture of courtesy and pomp. The judge tells an uplifting story about a woman from St. Croix, a maid whom she has known for many years and who is becoming a citizen that day. We raise our right hands. We renounce our allegiance to other nations, kings, potentates. We are led in the Pledge of Allegiance, right hands raised, odors of stinky cheese and turnips mingling in the air. I seem to be the only one who actually knows the words.

The judge leaves and the courtroom breaks out in chaos again. A team of INS officers yells out the names of the new Americans: Anatole, Bong-Su, Ying, Rasool, Sengupta.

I am craving a shower. I run out in the daylight and I hear one of your refrains. It makes me laugh because it's so facile, and I don't really think you believed it, but you liked telling me anyway: "I take my home with me where I go."

# SOME OF MY BEST FRIENDS

## Suheir Hammad

below their crisp skin
but above the pulse
they bear the numbers
inked onto their ancestors
who chant in their blood never
again never

they own their own names

they bring rugelach into
my home and share stories
of kids pulling hats in
search of horns

we cry and laugh
together in one breath

we look for each
other in crowds of flags
loud speakers who silence
us our solidarity angers

others who would always
rather war

when we do we
argue with each other the way
we do within our selves
fiercely with the security
of knowing love
is larger than our details

these are my people
and we are chosen
family eating darkness
hiccuping light little
by little by light
by little by light
together

# ABOUT THE
# CONTRIBUTORS

ELIZABETH ALEXANDER is the author of three books of poems, *The Venus Hottentot, Body of Life,* and *Antebellum Dream Book,* and a collection of essays, *The Black Interior.* Her poetry and prose have been collected in dozens of anthologies. Alexander has taught at Haverford College, the University of Chicago, Smith College, and New York University, and she has received grants from the National Endowment for the Arts and Guggenheim Foundation, as well as the Quantrell Award for Excellence in Undergraduate Teaching. She is on the faculty of Yale University and lives in New Haven, Connecticut.

BILL AYERS is Distinguished Professor of Education and Senior University Scholar at the University of Illinois at Chicago, and author of several books, including a memoir, *Fugitive Days.*

MAURICE BERGER is a Fellow at the Vera List Center for Art and Politics of the New School for Social Research in New York and Curator of the Center for Art and Visual Culture, University of Maryland, Baltimore County. His articles have appeared in many journals and newspapers, including *Artforum, Art in America,* the *New York Times,* the *Village Voice, October, Wired,* and the *Los Angeles*

*Times*. He is the author of the critically acclaimed *White Lies: Race and the Myths of Whiteness*—which was named as a finalist for the 2000 Horace Mann Bond Book Award of Harvard University and is being adapted as a television documentary for PBS—and six other books, including *How Art Becomes History*, *Constructing Masculinity*, *The Crisis of Criticism*, and *Postmodernism: A Virtual Discussion*.

EMILY BERNARD is the recipient of a fellowship from the National Endowment for the Humanities. An Assistant Professor of English and ALANA U.S. Ethnic Studies at the University of Vermont, Bernard is the editor of *Remember Me to Harlem: The Letters of Langston Hughes and Carl Van Vechten, 1925–1964*.

MICHELLE CLIFF is the author of the novels *Abeng, No Telephone to Heaven*, and *Free Enterprise*, and the short-story collections *Bodies of Water* and *The Store of a Million Items*.

TREY ELLIS is a novelist, screenwriter, and essayist. His acclaimed first novel, *Platitudes*, was recently reissued by Northeastern University Press along with his ground-breaking essay "The New Black Aesthetic," in a 1989 issue of *Callaloo*, an African Diaspora literary journal. He is also the author of *Home Repairs* and *Right Here, Right Now*, which was a recipient of the American Book Award. His work for the screen includes the Emmy-nominated *Tuskegee Airmen* and *Good Fences*, starring Danny Glover and Whoopi Goldberg. He lives in Venice, California, and in Paris.

JOHN GENNARI teaches English and ethnic studies at the University of Vermont. His book *Canonizing Jazz: An American Art and Its Critics* is forthcoming from the University of Chicago Press. His next book project is tentatively titled *Passing for Italian, Passing for Black: Crooners and Gangsters in Crossover Culture*. His essay on the black Italian actor Giancarlo Esposito appears in the collection *Are Italians White? How Race Is Made in America*.

SANDRA GUZMÁN is an award-winning journalist and author of the critically acclaimed self-help book *The Latina's Bible: The Nueva Latina's Guide to Love, Family, Spirituality and La Vida* (Three Rivers Press, 2002). As the former editor-in-chief of *Latina* magazine, Guzmán began her career as a general assignment reporter at *El Diario/La Prensa*, New York's largest and oldest Spanish-language newspaper. She was a television producer at New York's top-rated morning show, *Good Day New York* (WNYW-Fox TV). She worked as an assignment manager and producer at Telemundo's evening news (WNJU-TV), where in 1995 she won an Emmy for *The Cuban Embargo (Embargo Contra Cuba)*, a half-hour groundbreaking special on the U.S. embargo against the island nation. It was the station's first News and Public Affairs Programming Emmy. Guzmán was born in Puerto Rico and raised in New Jersey.

SUHEIR HAMMAD is the author of "Born Palestinian, Born Black" and "Drops of This Story." Hammad's work has appeared in numerous anthologies and journals. An original writer and cast member of the Tony award–winning *Russell*

*Simmons Presents Def Poetry Jam on Broadway*, she has also appeared in the Peabody award–winning HBO series *Def Poetry Jam*. The daughter of Palestinian refugees, Hammad was raised in Brooklyn, New York.

PAM HOUSTON is the author of two collections of linked short stories, *Cowboys Are My Weakness*, which was the winner of the 1993 Western States Book Award and has been translated into nine languages, and *Waltzing the Cat*, which won the Willa Award for Contemporary Fiction. Her stories were selected for the 1999 volumes of *Best American Short Stories*, *The O. Henry Awards*, *The Pushcart Prize*, and *Best American Short Stories of the Century*. A collection of Houston's autobiographical essays about travel and home, *A Little More About Me*, was published by W. W. Norton in the fall of 1999. In 2002 her first stage play, *Tracking the Pleiades*, was produced in Colorado. *Sighthound*, her first novel, will be published by W. W. Norton in January 2005. Houston is the Director of Creative Writing at University of California, Davis.

JEE KIM, born in Korea and raised in Philly, has called New York home since 1991. A longtime activist in the racial justice and youth-organizing movements, Jee has served as senior editor at *Stress Magazine* and has worked with Active Element and CAAAV: Organizing Asian Communities. His first publishing fame came as editor of *Another World Is Possible* (AnotherWorldisPossible.net), a progressive 9/11 anthology. He recently edited *The Future 500*

(Future500.com), a directory of youth activism in the United States, and is currently finishing his first novel, *Wreckless*.

DAVID MURA is the author of two memoirs, *Turning Japanese: Memoirs of a Sansei*, and *Where the Body Meets Memory: An Odyssey of Race, Sexuality and Identity*. He has also written two books of poetry, *After We Lost Our Way* and *The Colors of Desire*. His third book of poetry, *Angels for the Burning*, will be published by Boa Editions in 2004. His most recent book is *Song for Uncle Tom, Tonto and Mr. Moto*, a collection of literary criticism. He lives in Minneapolis.

DARRYL PINCKNEY is the author of a novel, *High Cotton*, and a frequent contributor to the *New York Review of Books*. He lives in New York and Oxford, England.

LUIS RODRIGUEZ is the award-winning author of eight books, including poetry, memoir, nonfiction, children's literature, and fiction. He is a cofounder of Tia Chucha's Café Cultural—a bookstore, café, art gallery, and performance space in the northeast San Fernando Valley section of LA. Check out his website for more information: www.luisjrodriguez.com.

SOMINI SENGUPTA was born in Calcutta, India, and raised in various unheralded towns and suburbs in Midwestern Canada and Southern California. She majored in English at UC Berkeley and worked as cocktail waitress, radio producer, and community organizer before stumbling onto journalism. At the *New York Times*, Sengupta has covered various beats (education, immigration, the 2000 presidential election row) before being named West Africa Bureau Chief in January 2003. She now trolls twenty-five countries in West and Central Africa in search of stories— never traveling without her lucky hat.

SUSAN STRAIGHT has published five novels. Her most recent novel, *Highwire Moon*, was a finalist for the National Book Award and received the Commonwealth of California Gold Medal for Fiction. Straight has published essays and articles in numerous magazines and journals, including the *New York Times*, *Harper's*, and *Salon*. Her short fiction has appeared in *Zoetrope All-Story*, *TriQuarterly*, *Story*, *Ploughshares*, the *Ontario Review*, and *North American Review*. Her short story "Mines" was chosen for *Best American Short Stories 2003* and won a Pushcart Prize in Fiction. Her commentaries are frequently heard on National Public Radio's *All Things Considered*. Susan Straight was born in Riverside, California, in 1960, and still lives there with her three daughters.